MW01256790

A Second Look

Encountering *the True Jesus*

A SECOND LOOK

ENCOUNTERING *THE TRUE JESUS*

Mark Hart

Our Sunday Visitor Publishing Division
Our Sunday Visitor, Inc.
Huntington, Indiana 46750

Nihil Obstat
Msgr. Michael Heintz, Ph.D.
Censor Librorum

Imprimatur
✠ Kevin C. Rhoades
Bishop of Fort Wayne-South Bend
October 5, 2015

The ***Nihil Obstat*** and ***Imprimatur*** are official declarations that a book is free from doctrinal or moral error. It is not implied that those who have granted the ***Nihil Obstat*** and ***Imprimatur*** agree with the contents, opinions, or statements expressed.

The Scripture citations used in this work are taken from the ***Catholic Edition of the Revised Standard Version of the Bible*** (RSV), copyright © 1965 and 1966 by the National Council of the Churches of Christ in the United States of America. Used by permission. All rights reserved.

Every reasonable effort has been made to determine copyright holders of excerpted materials and to secure permissions as needed. If any copyrighted materials have been inadvertently used in this work without proper credit being given in one form or another, please notify Our Sunday Visitor in writing so that future printings of this work may be corrected accordingly.

Copyright © 2016 by Mark Hart. Published 2016.

21 20 19 18 17 16 1 2 3 4 5 6 7 8 9

All rights reserved. With the exception of short excerpts for critical reviews, no part of this work may be reproduced or transmitted in any form or by any means whatsoever without permission from the publisher. For more information, visit: www.osv.com/permissions

Our Sunday Visitor Publishing Division, Our Sunday Visitor, Inc., 200 Noll Plaza, Huntington, IN 46750; 1-800-348-2440

ISBN: 978-1-61278-812-8 (Inventory No. T1618)
eISBN: 978-1-61278-372-7
LCCN: 2015957273

Cover design: Lindsey Riesen

PRINTED IN THE UNITED STATES OF AMERICA

Special thanks:

To Bert Ghezzi for his encouragement to "start writing" so many years ago, and for giving the Holy Spirit yet another opportunity to "wreck me" with His love and His Gospel.

To Rachel Peñate (for her holy editorial eye and worn-out backspace key), without whom the world would be forced to endure an unfathomable amount of parentheses, hyphens and constant ellipses flowing forth from my keyboard …

To Father Bob Schreiner for helping me sort out Spirit-led inspiration from personal assumption, and for reintroducing me to the beauty of the mystics.

To my gorgeous wife, Melanie, who repeatedly shows me the face of Christ's mercy, forgiveness, and compassion in our daily walk.

It would take a library of books to express my love and appreciation for you and, even then, simple words would not suffice.

You are the greatest gift the Lord has ever entrusted to me.

Thank you for the unseen sacrifices you make — and for helping me to become the man God calls me to be.

~

To our beautiful and incredible children: Hope, Faith, Trinity, and Josiah.

May you pursue the Lord with boldness, approach Him in humility, embrace Him with passion, and worship Him with abandon.

You four have taught me more about the love of the Father than any saint could ever hope to do. Thank you for the privilege of calling myself your daddy.

CONTENTS

Introduction

Life's Longest Journey

The road from your head to your heart is the longest journey you'll ever take.

You could be a platinum-status world traveler. You could backpack across South America. You could walk the 500-plus-mile *Camino* across Spain. You could even sail around the world. But, in the end, you will not have accomplished as much as the soul who comes to know himself in light of knowing the one, true God. This incredible journey from head to heart may take years, even decades, but it's the most important walk you'll ever take as a Christian and, indeed, as a human — where God goes from an "if" or a "what" to a "Who" … from a "power" to a Lover, from a teacher to a Savior.

Coming to "know" God in this way is not easy, but it is simple. Relationships require effort, and intimate relationships necessitate even more. Plenty of people know "about" Jesus, but even with the proliferation of technology and social media, fewer and fewer seem to truly know Him. Bibles go unread and prayers unsaid. Many of us function more off our pastor's view of God — or even Hollywood producers', political pundits', or atheist bloggers' views — than our own. Our vision or version of God is more often formed by others' opinions than transformed by a personal relationship with Truth Incarnate.

In this book you are going to be reintroduced to a handful of Bible characters and saints, and their individual stories. Some you might know well. Others you might not recognize at all. Some are heroic. Some are heartbreaking. But they're all thoroughly human. If you look hard enough, you might find a little bit of yourself in each story. At the very least, you'll be given an introduction to a God who is shocking and controversial, and uncontrollable in how He loves us. Perhaps this book will function as a reintroduction of sorts not only to the Gospels and the saints but to the Son of Man himself.

To be clear, I don't claim to have all the answers. In fact, this sinner doesn't claim to have any answer, save one … that Jesus Christ wants all of your heart, and the Good Shepherd is coming for you. You can run — plenty have — but He won't stop, and He won't relent. The sheep can't outrun the Good Shepherd. He'll climb the mountain and plunge deep into the ravine. He'll brave the hottest days and the coldest nights. He'll go without food and water, without sleep or rest. He'll leave the ninety-nine free to roam the hills. He'll never quit and never tire. He's coming after every sheep that wanders because you are worth more to Him than anything else.

The truth is that our God wants our hearts. Jesus Christ wants your heart, and He won't stop until He has it.

Christ came to save us, and we need to let Him. He didn't just come to teach us or to forgive us or to heal us (though He did all of those things); the itinerant carpenter from Nazareth came to save us. Jesus Christ may be meek, but *He is not weak*. He may be a lover, but He is also a warrior, one who has come to destroy death, conquer sin, and rescue us … often, from ourselves.

Good *versus* evil through Scripture

Every great story has a hero and a villain. Sometimes the greatest battles we wage are within ourselves. The enemy can be an external force, like an army, a giant, or a monster ... or the enemy can be internal. The animal we attempt to tame can often come from within ourselves.

Consistent through it all, though, are heroes. A hero cannot be measured by gender or in stature. A hero is not judged by intelligence or education, or by athletic ability or mere physical strength. No, a hero is judged by his or her heart.

Out of the Midian desert, the hero came as an elderly shepherd sent to take on a mighty Pharaoh; his name was Moses. On the plains outside Bethlehem, a hero came in the form of a teenager with a sling and five stones to battle a giant named Goliath; this teen was named David. From eastern France emerged a young peasant girl during the Hundred Years' War, a hero who would lead the French army to victories; she was named Joan. On the diseased and starving streets of Calcutta, a hero came in the form of a saintly woman less than five feet tall; her name was Teresa.

And under the veil of night beneath Bethlehem's sky, a hero came to us as a baby in a manger. Consider that premise. Is there any being on earth more beautiful or more gentle than a tiny baby? *This* was God's plan to save us from the enemy? *This* was our "mighty savior" lying in a trough?

Yes, our hope for salvation was pinned to the kid Mary was pinning diapers on. How's that for a great story? As if that weren't enough, throw in ancient prophecies, angelic interventions, a third-trimester road trip, a homicidal king, some dumbfounded shepherds, a few camel-lagged magi, and a birth announcement the size of a star, and you've got yourself a story better than anything Hollywood could dream of writing.

Some dismiss it as just "a nice story," but to do so is dangerous. The reality of God becoming man to save us from sin is far from a "nice" story. Sure, the baby Jesus is a gentle giant in the manger, but the events that preceded and followed are anything but pleasant. These mysteries — as they occurred — weren't actually all that "joyful."

In the pages to follow, salvation will unfold before you. It's a classic story with a hero and an enemy, a tale of good versus evil, of Light arriving, encountering, and eclipsing all darkness, one broken and remade heart at a time. It is now that God wants to remind you not only that He took flesh for you but that He died for you, *is fighting for you,* and has prepared a place in heaven for you.

Let's journey with the Lord through the Scriptures and watch His response to different sins and the souls who commit them. We will draw close to the Lord and peer deeply into His eyes. We're going to sit at His feet as wisdom falls from his lips. We're going to behold His face. We're going to incline our ears to timeless stories, but examine how they might be lived out in timely, twenty-first-century ways.

Every true journey begins with a question

Before you turn this page, though, ask yourself if you are willing to let the Lord love you in radical and frightening new ways. Are you willing to be challenged? Are you willing to let the Lord change you from the inside out? Are you willing to be uncomfortable? Are you willing to die to yourself, your plans, and your dreams if God calls you to it? Exactly how far are you willing to go for your God?

Are you willing to take *a second look* at the Jesus you currently know and allow Him to speak into your life in exciting and daunting new ways? Will you let the Lord love you in frightening new ways?

These are just a few of the questions we'll ponder, for if you're going to live as a Catholic Christian in the modern age … *get comfortable with being uncomfortable*. The cross reminds us that God would literally rather die than spend eternity without you. God could live without you — He just doesn't want to. God wants your heart, and by turning this page, you are signing the consent form.

The secret to a joyful life and a hope-filled future isn't about figuring out tomorrow; it's about listening to God today. God, the Author of Life, has something to say to you through the brothers and sisters who came before you.

Commit to read the biblical passages and verses referred to herein and to entering into the chapter challenges that follow. Do so and you will transform your homes, schools, workplaces, and parishes. You will breathe His light into others' darkness, and there is no more important gift you can help give than the gift of His salvation.

So, pray with me now, that our hearts would be open, our minds humble, and our souls thirsty:

Holy Spirit, be with us now. Direct our eyes to Christ and our hearts to the Father. Blessed Mother, swaddle us tightly with each turn of the page. Hold us close to your immaculate heart as you did your baby son and your crucified Lord.

Come, Holy Spirit... Come, Holy Spirit...
Come, Holy Spirit. Amen.

Now, let's take a walk.

Chapter 1

Encountering Jesus Calls You to More

Christ and the Magi

We have five Nativity sets in my house: not out of overindulgence, but out of sheer necessity. One set is for my one-year-old, who is still learning how to treat things gently and that the horns of an ox are not to be used as a weapon. One set is for my six-year-old, who likes to take a more "interactive" approach to the Nativity, including inserting Disney princesses and Barbies into the biblical narrative. Last year, when I asked why the baby Jesus was in Barbie's convertible, she responded, "Barbie is baby-sitting, Daddy … the trip to Bethlehem left Mary and Joseph very tired."

The third set is for my nine-year-old. She doesn't want anyone "messing up" the set by placing the figures the wrong way or in the incorrect order. The fourth set is for my "tween" who enjoys retelling the Nativity story from each character's unique perspective … oftentimes adding accents to their voices. I'm not sure why the angels have an English accent in her brain, but the Gloria sounds classy, so I'm okay with it. The last is one very nice ceramic Nativity set high atop a bookshelf that my wife and I gaze upon and patrol diligently due to its fragility. A closer examination will reveal the angel has only one hand and the lamb only three legs, due to the "incidents" of 2007 and 2009, respectively (which again explains why it now sits up so high).

Each set represents something special and important. As a father, *I want my children to place themselves in the story*. It is essential that they see the birth of Christ as meaningful and fundamentally important in their own lives. And as sons and daughters of God, you and I need to remember the same thing.

It's easy, though, for this to become just a story, isn't it? It's romantic and sacred and somehow almost too good to be true. This reality is a dangerous one. When we begin to view biblical truths through a purely historical lens, we lose something essential. Sometimes it's healthy to re-imagine the scene again. As St. Francis (who gave us the first crèche) might suggest, picture the Nativity not as a set of figurines displayed on an end table, but rather as living, breathing souls huddled amidst the animals in a dimly lit cave on a cold winter's night.

Inspired by grace

Swaddled tightly beneath a star-blanketed Bethlehem sky, God breathed gently yet powerfully. The acceptable time had come. The prophecies were now — at last — fulfilled. The Creator had invaded His creation on a mission of love and, for the next three decades, peace and joy would be breathed and "inhaled" (received) in tangible new ways.

That night, the divine life of God was communicated through a tiny human breath. Put simply, God breathed not solely so that He might live but that we would. It's fascinating how something so small, a breath, roughly eight ounces of oxygen, forms the line between life and death.

The Latin word for breath — *inspirare* — is where we get the term "inspiration"; it literally means, "to breathe [life] into." Inspiration, however, is far more than a biological word or concept; it is a deeply spiritual reality. *God's inspiration animates our Christian souls, guides our steps, and offers us both a mission and a purpose.* We talk about how the Bible is the "inspiration" of the Holy Spirit … the Word of God through the pens of men. Stop and consider how vital this inspiration of God is to our faith and, indeed, our lives as Catholics! The Church is inspired, the sacraments are inspired, and — with any luck — with every encounter we witness on the pages of sacred Scripture we, too, are inspired. We breathe in God's life (grace) that we might share it. Inspiration leads to respiration.

When we begin to view biblical truths through a purely historical lens, we lose something essential.

Since you began reading this you've probably taken between twenty and thirty breaths (fifty if you're reading it on a treadmill, which isn't safe, but hamsters applaud your effort). We know, of course, that inspiration is vital not only for our bodies but also for our souls. It's when we realize how desperately we need oxygen that we come to appreciate it more.

It's how our story began, after all (or, "before all," if you want to get technical). Life began because God spoke; He breathed the word (see Gn 1:3) and creation spun into existence. It was when God breathed life into Adam, however, that things got even more interesting (Gn 2:7). Creation now bore the ability to inspire: to procreate life in God's image.

We often speak about the people and the things that inspire us — heroic characters, timeless tales — heart-stopping and soul-stirring moments that ironically bring us life by taking our breath away. Authentic inspiration is a gift from God, the giver of all good and perfect gifts (see Jas 1:17).

Now would be a good time to take a deep breath, actually, because throughout the sacred Scriptures (also, *inspired* by the Spirit's breath) you might notice that rarely does anything life-changing or soul-altering occur in a primary character until *after* God has moved them. Looking back, you might come to find the same rings true in your own life.

Abram and his family were moved well over 2,500 miles before God revealed the patriarch's true mission. Moses was a murderer hiding in the desert wilderness before God called him back to Egypt and, then, on to Sinai and the Promised Land. Joshua fled. Elijah ran. Esther's family was deported into captivity. Even Jeremiah, though left behind in an increasingly desolated Jerusalem during the Babylonian capture, was "moved" from his comfort zone to a prophetic life of deep sorrow and eventual peace. God often moves those He loves to create more "space" for Him, to shake us free from created things (see Heb 12:26) and leave only what is unshaken (Heb 12:27).

What does this mean for you and me, personally? It means that God is the irresistible force often trying to call us immovable objects forward; the Father desires the ill-tempered brats to become malleable children.

Ask yourself: "Has God been trying to *move me*? Has the Father been trying to get this child's attention and, if so, have I actually listened, or have I put in the 'earbuds' of modern busyness, stress, overwork, and self-involvement?"

If we want to see Jesus, we have to take our eyes out of our navels and peer *up* into the heavens.

Grand reopening

Have you ever driven by the "Grand Opening" of a restaurant or store? Oftentimes, you'll see those giant moving spotlights out front, casting rays of blinding light into the night sky. The lights are designed to catch our attention, to announce something big, and to draw customers closer. Our human eyes are even more captivated by the mechanical lights shining up from earth than the light emanating down from the stars, stars that our ancestors affectionately called "the heavens."

Our hearts are often drawn to artificial "lights" the world has to offer. We seek earthly solutions to our heavenly desires. Some people run to food and others to drugs. Some run to relationships and others to screens. Some people's artificial light is popularity, and for others it is money. There is an endless list of diversions and quick fixes, but *nothing external can heal the void internal.* It takes Christ. He is our healer and savior. He is the solution to our problem of sin. Jesus is both the surgeon and the solution; His very life (which we call "grace") is our antidote.

Look at the star of Bethlehem, for instance — even the celestial orb rising in the heavens functioned only as an arrow, an announcement … an external *symbol.* The star served as a starting point of the Magi's journey and — by extension — our own. As it's been said countless times before, wise men *still seek Him*. The external star symbolizes something that resides deep within us all, an internal longing for heaven's glory. The pursuit of the Wise Men is reminiscent of our own pursuit of God. Something begins to happen within us when we admit our sinfulness and seek Jesus with more intensity. Literally, the mystery of Christ moves us and the love of Christ impels (and then propels) us forward.

I often wonder if I would have traveled as far for Christ as the Magi did. I mean, I only have to drive fifteen minutes to my parish to encounter the King of Kings in the tabernacle, upon the altar, in the adoration chapel or confessional. The Magi saddled dromedaries and headed west for the greatest road trip recorded in the Bible. I get stressed corralling four kids and my lovely bride into the car and then the pew before the entrance hymn is completed. But, the Wise Men journeyed for months, on a whim and a star. That's faith. That is the kind of reckless abandon that all modern Christians need but few seem to possess, myself very much included.

Three wise guys and a baby

About twelve days after Christmas (you might recognize that time frame from the song) we celebrate the feast of the Epiphany, focusing on the events following Christ's birth, when the Magi arrived and worshiped the King of Kings. While they didn't RSVP for this baby shower, it's difficult to imagine Mary or Joseph would have complained, especially when they carried in the gifts they did — gold, frankincense, and myrrh weren't cheap (and not easily purchased from their local Target). When the "wise men" parked their camels and fell on their knees, their act of worship revealed something amazing: good news that would impact us all.

St. Matthew details the encounter for us:

> When they had heard the king they went their way; and lo, the star which they had seen in the East went before them, till it came to rest over the place where the child was. When they saw the star, they rejoiced exceedingly with great joy; and going into the house they saw the child with Mary his mother, and they fell

> down and worshiped him. Then, opening their treasures, they offered him gifts, gold and frankincense and myrrh." (Matthew 2:9-11)

Envision this miraculous encounter. The star they had followed now came to rest, the light shining in darkness now showered light upon the Light of the world. God from God, light from light, true God from true God. Here lay a baby — born and begotten, though not made — so radiant in splendor that the hearts of learned minds became so full they fell to their knees. Picture Mary's expression in this moment. They all knew the prophecy, but Mary held the prophet. The shepherds had come and found the Lamb (of God) … now the Wise Men came and found Wisdom Incarnate.

Picture the baby Jesus. Is He squirming or calm? How is Mary holding Him? Did He wail before the Magi or laugh? Were they allowed to hold the one who held the universe in His tiny hands? Did they kiss His brow? Was He bathed in their tears? Imagine the validation they must have felt after such a journey — *not* a validation that they were right, but that they had now encountered all that is right in the universe.

The shepherds had come and found the Lamb (of God) … now the Wise Men came and found Wisdom Incarnate.

If you've ever experienced pure love, you know how it ruins you for anything less. The Magi not only experienced their Creator but sat in the presence of the only soul the Creator chose to need so profoundly … the blessed Mother. There is no way, once you behold the splendor of God so simply, that the simple ever looks the same again. As Fyodor Dostoyevsky said: "If you love ... you will perceive the divine mystery in things. Once you perceive it, you will begin to comprehend it better every day" (*The Brothers Karamazov*).

Imagine how impressive the gold would have looked to the Magi on the way to Bethlehem, and how it paled in comparison to the luminance emanating from the manger upon their arrival. How shiny the gold, how thick the cloud of incense, how fragrant the myrrh — all overshadowed by the God of the universe — the Bread of Life — laid in a feedbox. Consider how the things of the world can appear so impressive and pressing at times, occupying all of our thought and stressing our senses. They're stressful, that is, until we are in the presence of God — Christ's true presence in the Eucharist — where heaven kisses earth, once again, in gentleness and in mercy, just as it did in Bethlehem.

Moving forward from Bethlehem

Tradition reveals that the names of the Magi are Gaspar, Melchior, and Balthazar. Though no one knows for sure, it was St. Bede the Venerable (672-735) who filled in the details on the Wise Men, teaching:

- Melchior was an older man, with a long white beard and white hair, who brought gold to celebrate the kingship of Jesus.
- Gaspar was a younger, beardless, and "ruddy" (red-haired) man who offered (frank)incense to honor the divinity of Christ.
- Balthazar was a middle-aged man of black complexion, with a heavy beard, who offered myrrh to signify the humanity of the Lord.

Medieval legends state that their bones were put in the cathedral of Cologne, the "City of the Three Kings," brought there in 1164. Originally, they were considered and depicted as astrologers, but about the Middle Ages or so the interpretation began to take on the notion more of "kings." Some traditions hold that St. Thomas the Apostle visited them later on in life, catechized and initiated them fully into the Christian faith, and that they were later ordained priests and bishops. So why do we still hail these three characters, immortalized in song and art, two thousand years later?

The word "epiphany" means "to reveal." This is where Jesus's identity would be revealed to the greater world, beyond Mary and Joseph, some shepherds, and the animals. When the Gentile (non-Jewish) astrologers roll in from the East, it's a signal that this blessed birth to a poor Jewish couple was going to affect far more people than just their immediate family; this holy baby's life would have effects on an international stage. The birth of Jesus had universal (or, in Greek, "catholic") implications. It is a bold and beautiful announcement that God's kingdom had, indeed, come, and when God's kingdom comes, our "kingdoms" must go. Regardless of what happened later, we must not forget the simplest lessons the Magi taught us: they showed up, worshiped Jesus, and brought their gifts. Ask yourself if you do all three. If not, "Why not?" And if so, keep it up.

It's easy, though, for the Epiphany to function as and remain a mere story to the twenty-first-century believer. So, what does this really mean for us today? Why are these characters — these "three kings" (even though Scripture lists only three gifts, not three people) — still being celebrated and sung about and made into tiny Nativity-set action figures? How does their action impact the modern believer?

There are several things we can learn from the Magi, actually. Consider, just a few:

- Sometimes God calls us to search for Him with our bodies and, indeed, with our whole heart. It may take time to "find" the Lord, but it is in the seeking that we come to yearn for Him even more. In seeking God, we actually come to realize that He is the One seeking us and calling out to us in signs and wonders right in front of us.

- True adoration and worship culminate and find their place at the manger. In modern settings, the manger is your parish altar/chapel, tabernacle, and/or monstrance. Bethlehem is not half a world away; it is as near as your home parish.
- Just as God offers us His physical presence (in Christ Jesus), we are invited to offer ourselves back to Him, along with our gifts, talents, etc. A gift is not a gift until it is freely given … until then it is a possession.
- We are all invited to encounter God and to receive His grace … no credentials except sin are necessary; current saints need not apply.
- The journey to Bethlehem took the Magi time and great effort. Their example should encourage you to ask yourself, "How *far* am I willing to go for Christ?" What more does God have to do to prove His love beyond the Cross, His mercy beyond absolution, and His intimacy beyond the sacraments?
- Are you willing to lay down your gifts and your very lives in worship of God? That question sounds simple enough, but the simplest questions are often the most dangerous and the most difficult to answer.

Remember that the motivation and effort of your gift-giving is often far more meaningful than the gift itself. The Magi's trust — their travel, effort, and worship — far outshone the gifts that they bore. Still, today, far more meaningful than your mere physical presence in the church is the motivation behind it and the worship you unleash when in the Lord's presence.

The not-so-happy ending

In the midst of these — and many more lessons we can learn from the Epiphany — we can't forget the drama going on behind the scenes.

The Magi had encountered King Herod, who wanted to know the whereabouts of the newborn Christ. Threatened by ancient prophecies coming true, the bloodthirsty king wanted the baby dead. God had raised a star in the heavens, magi had traveled, Mary and Joseph had too, the inn was full, the angels had proclaimed, the shepherds visited, and just when things were supposed to calm down, it got even more dangerous. It took angelic intervention — fleeing the town under the veil of night, escaping the grip of a homicidal king, and returning to foreign lands — for the Holy Family and the blessed Magi to be safe and process all they had experienced.

This is no Disney movie. This is not the "happy ending" to the birth story, either. This is reality. This happened. This was another miraculous event in the historic battle between good and evil, where the light, once again, overcomes the darkness. These were real souls that journeyed, worshiped, adored, and eventually returned home, changed forever.

During the Epiphany, the epic saga of salvation history takes a dramatic and unexpected turn, announcing God's presence to a world desperately in need of it. Nothing much has changed. You are magi now, traveling to your local Bethlehem (parish), advancing toward a different-looking manger (the altar), and laying down your gifts and your life before the King each week. You make the trip physically, yes, but it's how far you are willing to go spiritually that makes a difference. Will you kneel? Will you worship? Will you allow the Lord to change you forever?

The answers to those questions will determine whether or not the faithful will be celebrating your life two thousand years from now when you are a saint. If your immediate response to that last sentence was "Me? A saint? Not a chance!" then may I submit your God is too small. No sin is greater than His mercy. No sin. God took flesh to save us from our sins. He gave us His Holy Spirit to help us become saints. The Holy Spirit's job is — quite literally — to make us holy.

The Christmas mystery — the mystery of the Incarnation — invites us to active prayer. God emptying himself and taking on flesh is beautiful, not only because of the humility and gentleness of the baby in the manger, but because of His invitation to interact with Him physically and intimately. *The entire Nativity scene is a celebration of God's love for His children*, His willingness to stop at nothing to ensure our salvation. It is a scene that we must prayerfully engage in, not just passively "admire." Never forget that the Lord didn't come to be admired, but to be worshiped. Fall on your knees this night, as they did so many centuries ago, and worship the God who loved you enough to be born into the world's filth and sin, to save you from it.

A Step Beyond

So how can we live out the reality of the Magi's journey in our own lives? How do we answer the call with similar abandon?

Ask God to reveal to you which people or things, fears or stresses inadvertently become your "god." You may want to compile a list of the things that occupy a majority of your thoughts instead of God. What are the stresses that render you distant when you're called to be present to family or friends? What are the anxieties that steal your focus and energy when you go to pray?

If you aren't sure "who your God is," you might want to begin with your social media profile. Who and what do you post about the most? Who occupies a majority of your thoughts and energy? If Christ was right (and He always is) when He said, "For where your treasure is, there will your heart be also" (Mt 6:21), then we can learn a lot from where we spend our time and energy.

No sin is greater than His mercy.

We cannot worship the true God until we acknowledge any false gods that have crept in and set up shop in our souls.

This self-assessment is challenging and humbling. It's thirsty work ... let's grab a drink.

Chapter 2

Encountering Jesus Unleashes God's Mercy

Christ and the Samaritan Woman

Hide-and-seek was my favorite game growing up. The strategy of securing the perfect hiding place, the thrill of the countdown, the heart-stopping anxiety that my six-year-old body endured, the frantic scurrying to hide and then holding my breath as I heard the seeker getting closer — it was almost too much pressure for my pre-adolescent heart to endure.

The lessons we learn from hide-and-seek are lessons we can carry with us throughout life: the importance of thinking under pressure, the integrity necessary to keep our eyes closed while counting, the ability to remain silent for long periods of time, and the joy derived from taking a break to play a game with friends. But, the takeaways aren't just practical applications of moral development. The game offers a fundamental look at a timeless theological "dilemma" — namely, when it comes to God, are we really seeking Him, or is He the one seeking us?

No more games

Too often we treat our relationship with God like a game of hide-and-seek … at least, I do. At times I run from Him. At times I try to hide from Him and act as though He cannot see me. At times I even hold my breath and don't talk to Him, hoping He won't find me. The painful truth is that I almost think, if He can't find me, He can't ask me to change.

There's just one obvious problem with this juvenile thought process: **We can't hide from God**.

To God everything is exposed: all of our faults, imperfections, and little personal secrets. But God knows everything: all of our talents, traits, successes, and achievements — that's the good news. *The even better news* is that God is always seeking you and me: "For the Son of Man came to seek and to save the lost" (Lk 19:10). Ponder that Gospel truth for a minute, because it's life altering. You might never miss Mass. You may constantly be reading different spiritual books about the Lord such as this one. You could have a disciplined — even vibrant — prayer life. The radio stations in your car could be preprogrammed to Catholic or Christian stations. You could wake up each day "seeking" the Lord and to grow in your faith. But, the soul-stirring reality is that it's actually the other way around. You're not seeking God even a fraction as much as God is seeking you. God doesn't stop, either. He doesn't want "part" of your heart, or life, or strength. No, God wants it all. He wants all of your heart, and He's not going to relent. Christ won't stop until you place your heart into His splintered and nail-scarred hands.

Jesus is the Good Shepherd, the one who goes out of His way for each of us silly, lost sheep. No sin is too great for this Savior; no lamb is worth losing to this Lord. He isn't afraid of your past sins, current status, or social structure. We have a God who constantly draws near to where we are to bring us to where He is. The Living Water is flowing, and peering into Christ's eyes reveals the dehydration of our souls.

A woman, a well, and a wish

One could only imagine the types of insults that were uttered about the woman at the well. So many ex-husbands would have left few souls in such a tiny village at a loss for words. The Samaritan woman we hear about in St. John's Gospel would have been a small-town gossip's dream. She is the type of soul few would expect much from, except sin, that is. No one wanted to engage a woman such as this. Certainly no prophet or respectable preacher would be seen in her presence, much less engaging her in dialogue.

Christ won't stop until you place your heart into His splintered and nail-scarred hands.

Our Lord Jesus does precisely that, however, for when the Living Word draws near, He doesn't see the sin; He sees the sinner in need of God's mercy. In fact, the conversation between Christ and the woman at the well is the longest recorded dialogue Jesus has with one person in any of the Gospels. That fact alone ought to cause us pause and intrigue us to read the episode again, with fresh eyes and an open heart. The Holy Spirit inspired these words not for us to view them as a third-person "reader" but as a first-person "sinner" … for as the Lord seeks her, He is seeking us just as fervently:

> Now when the Lord … left Judea and departed again to Galilee. He had to pass through Samaria. So he came to a city of Samaria, called Sychar, near the field that Jacob gave to his son Joseph. Jacob's well was there, and so Jesus, wearied as he was with his journey, sat down beside the well. It was about the sixth hour. (John 4:1,3-6)

It's vital to remember when reading sacred Scripture that no word is meaningless. God inspires every single word for a reason. Sometimes it's very evident. Other times we may gloss over a phrase without giving it a second thought, such as here when the Holy Spirit reveals, "He had to pass through Samaria."

Why is that so important? Is Jesus's preferred route of travel really significant two thousand years later? Scriptural details are an invitation to go deeper into the mind and heart of God. Obviously, the Spirit wanted us to know this fact, so what are we to take from it?

In the time of Jesus, Jews and Samaritans didn't interact with one another. There was a deep-seated hatred between them extending far beyond any Democrat/Republican dislike or even the Yankees and Red Sox vitriol. A Jew quite simply didn't go into Samaria if he could avoid it. There were alternate (though, far longer) routes around the region that were preferable. Even if it were a searing hot desert day and you wanted to take the most direct route, if it meant you (a good Jew) had to interact with a Samaritan, you would go miles out of your way just to avoid the cultural disgust and social stigma. The best-case scenario meant a Jew wouldn't have to see Samaritans, talk to them, or interact with them on any level. Try telling that to the God of the universe.

The carpenter from Nazareth was anything but politically correct. Christ paid no attention to cultural bias or racial tension. Repeatedly throughout the Gospels we see Our Lord shattering social norms. To put it simply, He had a divine appointment that day at the well, unbeknownst to the Samaritan woman fetching water.

We're told by St. John that it was "about the sixth hour" of the day, making it about high noon for us twenty-first-century readers not savvy about Mediterranean and Hebraic timekeeping. Another seemingly unnecessary detail that offers intriguing insight into the woman's cultural standing: Why would she go to the well at high noon? Why not earlier in the morning or right before sunset, when either time would offer cooler temperatures? You do not go to the well at the hottest part of the day without a reason.

The well was the proverbial "water cooler" of two thousand years ago. It was where everyone in the village would congregate and the best gossip would occur. Those desiring community (and social gab) would go at sundown, typically. Some biblical scholars and saints even offer that this woman went there at noon because she had a sordid reputation; this woman ventured out for a laborious task in the heat of the day just to avoid the crowds who judged and ridiculed her. Luckily for the woman, her past did not dictate her future … not with a God so limitless in compassion, one who breathes divine mercy. It was high noon, yes — the brightest part of the day — and it was against this backdrop, with everything exposed and nowhere to hide, that God came seeking:

> There came a woman of Samaria to draw water. Jesus said to her, "Give me a drink." For his disciples had gone away into the city to buy food. The Samaritan woman said to him, "How is it that you, a Jew, ask a

> drink of me, a woman of Samaria?" For Jews have no dealings with Samaritans. Jesus answered her, "If you knew the gift of God, and who it is that is saying to you, 'Give me a drink,' you would have asked him and he would have given you living water." The woman said to him, "Sir, you have nothing to draw with, and the well is deep; where do you get that living water?" (John 4:7-11)

Of course, this scene presented yet another problem. Not only did Jews and Samaritans not "mix," but also, at the time, men and women would certainly not interact with one another in public — and under no circumstances would they share a drink or a cup. And, if a woman had a sinful reputation, a prophet — a true prophet and man of honor — would assuredly not engage or associate with her because of her sinful stature. This type of interaction would have been overtly scandalous and unheard of. Yet this Jesus sat completely present to the "sinner," unfazed by her past but deeply interested in her future.

And not only does Jesus break convention and draw near to her in public, not only does He talk to her, but He asks for a drink from her!?! Why on God's earth would He do such a scandalous thing?

Simple: the living water thirsted for her salvation.

The only other time we hear Jesus mention His thirst is while agonizing on the cross. His agony was internal on this day as God's deepest desire was to free this woman from her personal sins. In a way, this episode, beside the well, foreshadows the Cross. The thirst Jesus acknowledges here foreshadows the thirst He will reveal later. The mercy He offers in a cup for one beside a well prefigures the mercy offered in the cup for the many in the Upper Room, in Gethsemane's garden, and upon Calvary's stony hill.

> Jesus said to her, "Every one who drinks of this water will thirst again, but whoever drinks of the water that I shall give him will never thirst; the water that I shall give him will become in him a spring of water welling up to eternal life." The woman said to him, "Sir, give me this water, that I may not thirst, nor come here to draw." (John 4:13-15)

We all thirst. We are born with it. It's a scientific and physiological fact that humans can go longer without food than they can without water. What does this physical need have to do with one's prayer life, though? Why so much talk about water and life in a biblical chapter or spiritual book about God? Put simply, this discussion between the woman and Jesus is still hashed out every day with modern believers and those who want to believe but struggle (or outright refuse) to do so. The need for spiritual water is a matter of life and death whether people understand it or not.

It is not until you encounter the living water from heaven that you truly begin to realize just how parched your life on earth has become.

Do you know what prayer does? Do you realize what worshiping God does? Do you fully understand what adoration and the sacraments do? Among other things, these encounters with God, these forms of prayer *reveal the dehydration of our souls.*

It is not until you encounter the living water from heaven that you truly begin to realize just how parched your life on earth has become. Christ, though, is far more than a canteen for emergencies in the arid deserts of our self-involved existence. Our Lord is more than an oasis in which to seek respite in times of survival. God is far more, and He is inviting us to far more. He has revealed this to us through a midday conversation at the local watering hole. God invited this woman — and us — to dive into the ocean of His mercy and finally experience what freedom tastes like.

The taste of freedom

Encountering God is a dangerous venture. It's as though we know we need Him but aren't quite sure we're ready for Him or all that listening to Him will entail. We want God around. Sure. Why not? He's like that lucky rabbit's foot. We might not invoke Him enough before we really need Him, but when the going gets tough, we invoke God plenty. We have Him there for safe measure. He's my "divine life insurance," and that's a great deal! I mean, most of us live with the perfect plan for how and when we'll "let God in." It's as though we are saying, "God, when you call me home, please make it so I'm on a deathbed surrounded by priests throwing holy water and oil on me, hearing my confession, and making sure I get to your home address quickly and without any stops." Sadly, it doesn't always work that way.

Jesus could have taken the long route. Our Lord could have opted to go the long way around, sure. He didn't then, and He still doesn't. Remember, "Jesus Christ is the same yesterday and today and for ever" (Heb 13:8). Jesus didn't oppose the sinner, then, and He sure as heaven isn't going to oppose you now.

Christ didn't leave us to figure out truth, repentance, and forgiveness on our own. Jesus had a divine appointment, and He went straight to the place He wasn't supposed to go, to the person He wasn't supposed to talk with. *He wasn't revealing His thirst*; *He was inviting her to reveal hers!* As He talks to her, though, He reveals even more:

> Jesus said to her, "Go, call your husband, and come here." The woman answered him, "I have no husband." Jesus said to her, "You are right in saying, 'I have no husband'; for you have had five husbands, and he whom you now have is not your husband; this you said truly." The woman said to him, "Sir, I perceive that you are a prophet." (John 4:16-19)

So, the Lord takes this nice scene and, as with the tables in the Temple area, completely upends it. In a shocking moment ripe for reality television, Jesus reveals that not only has this woman had five husbands but that number six isn't even wed to her! This is where the dramatic music would be cued to alert the viewers of the scandal. Can you imagine how you'd feel — all of your sins hanging out in broad daylight, revealed by this seemingly random Nazarene carpenter/mystery man? All of a sudden, the Samaritan woman was face to face with the God of the universe and the reality of her own shame.

Some read this passage and think: "That's not right. How could God do such a thing to her? Isn't it bad enough that the Samaritan townspeople gossip about her, and then this random Jewish carpenter is going to come to call her out?" To be clear, though, that is *how much God loves her*. God revealed her sin precisely *because* of His unfathomable love. If He didn't say, "I know about your past," she would say, "Fooled him! He's no prophet." The fact is that He drew right next to her, looked her right in the eyes, and basically said, "I know about your shame, and I still love you." Jesus didn't want her to be chained to her sinful past any longer. God loved her so much that He crashed into her existence in an unsuspecting moment, not just to forgive her but to save her. He wants her to come face to face with her former self, not to rub her nose in it but in hopes that she will invite him into it!

What would your response be if you were the one holding the bucket? Would you deny the sin? Would you walk away? Would you possibly retaliate, firing back at the mystery man? Or would you own your past as you sat in a shame-filled present?

I have a confession to make

Do you know what happens when our sin is brought into the light? We either look for a place to hide it or seek a place to dump it. Therapy often wades through the former, while the Sacrament of Reconciliation beckons us to the latter. The woman beside the well looked Christ in the eyes as she was made new. We have the exact same opportunity thanks to Christ's priesthood here on earth.

Shoulders slumped from fatigue; eyes bloodshot; stoles a beautiful, albeit disgusting, blend of countless young souls' tears: This is a not-too-uncommon sight in youth ministry — that is, priests sitting *in persona Christi capitas* offering mercy and absolution to an endless line of adolescent sinners ardently desiring sainthood. The scene repeats itself at every parish retreat, summer camp, and youth rally. The numbers are staggering, with priests hearing on some weekends hundreds of confessions. These courageous (and tired) souls are consistently poured out like libations in a manner that would make St. Paul proud (see Phil 2:17), often remaining on less-than-comfortable chairs for hours on end so that every last penitent has the opportunity to hear the beautiful and incomparable words of freedom ... "I absolve you."

After a cursory glance around the room during these events, many are quick to blame the priest shortage (an irresponsible euphemism for what is really a "response shortage" — God is calling, men just aren't listening or hearing, but let's not digress). A more exacting evaluation would reveal a group of teens who have either not been offered the opportunity more frequently or, perhaps more to the point, have not been invited into the sacramental encounter since the last such retreat/event. The lines are long for a variety of reasons, but the ratio of teens to priests is not the fundamental problem; it's a fruit, but not the root. **The Church needs more sin**. Yes, you read that correctly. The Church needs more sin *to be preached and taught about*, so that we can be reconciled more regularly. Sin has not lost its luster; leaders have lost their muster. And that is one very deadly combination. Even in a suffering economy, the wages of sin remain the same: death (see Rom 6:23).

So, why don't leaders preach and teach more about sin? I believe it's rooted in fear. Sometimes leaders are afraid that preaching sin will push people away or hurt their numbers or, worst yet, their collection. Experience shows, however, that if done correctly, the result is just the opposite. Did the woman at the well retreat in fear or advance for mercy? Humble souls are dying for someone to draw a line in the sand. To quote G. K. Chesterton, "Art, like morality, consists in drawing a line somewhere."

Souls want truth; hearts are hard-wired for it. More to the point, everyone needs truth ... especially the truth about hell, heaven, purgatory, and the lives that lead to all three. Modern minds aren't stupid, nor should they be placated or pandered to. While always couched in compassion and mercy, God didn't shy away from preaching on truth, sin, and consequence; He began in Eden and continues to speak truth throughout salvation history. Even Christ's beloved Sermon on the Mount spoke more about hell and the consequence of sin than any of His other discourses or (far easier-to-remember) parables.

People have forgotten a fundamental truth about sin — namely, that God did not give Adam and Eve the right to decide subjectively what was good and evil; in His mercy, He gave them *the right to choose between what is objectively good and evil.* He was adamant. He was clear. He loved them (and us) enough not to leave anything in doubt. He explained the consequences (see Gn 2:17).

Today, souls are being swallowed up and spit out by a secular humanist, morally relativist culture. Taking ownership of our sin is not a popular thing to do, especially for Christians in the modern age. Most of the time, when we have a lot of sin and shame in our past, we prefer to pretend it's not there. We are happy to show God all the bright and shiny parts of our life, but prefer to keep the Lord out of the junk drawers and messy closets of our soul. Some have convinced themselves that their sins are anything but. No sin equals no need for a Savior. Though weighed down by the guilt, they'd rather breathe than really live, as their soul dies a painful death. The woman at the well wasn't really living … she was merely breathing, until "the way, and the truth, and the life" (Jn 14:6) offered her renewal.

Unless you reconcile the past, you're never going to taste the future God has designed for you.

Others are so overwhelmed by the gravity of their past sins that they won't even let God into their past. These souls desire God to be present in their present and merciful in their future, but they won't allow the Lord into their past. Though they might even live in their past, they are afraid to let Christ anywhere near it. These souls that dwell in the past go back every chance they get. "You can't forgive me, Lord. I've sinned too much and run too far. My sin, it's just too big," they think. They might even lament: "Church? Oh, I can't go to church. I can't go in … that place will fall down if I'm in it."

Allow me to say that if the Church hasn't fallen down in 2,000 years, it sure as hell is not going to fall down because of you. The Catholic Church is a Church of mercy; in fact, that's our mission statement. We are a Church who now counts former mass murderers, con artists, alcoholics, thieves, rapists, and heretics among the Communion of Saints. *Never doubt the power of God's grace nor the ability it affords you to change.*

If we don't say, "God, I don't just want you to be the God of my present or the God of my future, but I want you to be the God and savior of my past!" then we are missing Simon Peter's boat. Tell the Lord, now: "I want you to walk back with me, Jesus. I trust you. Please tell me I don't have to carry this anymore. Please forgive me. Please tell me You still love this sinner called Your child."

The only sin God will not forgive is the one you don't ask forgiveness for. So don't keep your past from Him. You can't be made new for today or tomorrow until you invite Jesus to redeem yesterday.

Wherever you're at, whether you've dealt with your past or you haven't, when the Lord comes to you and looks you in the eyes, He's not saying to you, "You are the sum of your sins and your failures." No, God's truth, to paraphrase words of St. John Paul II, is that you are not the sum of your sins, you are the sum of the Father's love. Unless you reconcile the past, you're never going to taste the future God has designed for you. If you keep throwing your bucket down that well of stagnant water, it's not going to fulfill your thirst as He is.

One of the greatest things you can do for your spiritual life is to say to Jesus in prayer: "Walk with me, Lord. Walk me back into this episode, sin, room, addiction, struggle [whatever it is]. Walk back with me and show me where You've preserved me and protected me. Reveal it to me, Lord. Pour light into my darkness. Show me where I need healing, Lord, and then please come and heal me. Come, Jesus, and save me from my darkness, my past, and myself."

The Lord reveals our shame because He loves us and wants to free us. The enemy reveals our shame because he wants to chain us and leave us there.

Samaria is half a world away, but the reality is that right now — possibly for the first time ever — Jesus wants you to stop and take a second look. Gaze into the eyes of mercy as if it is the first time you ever have. He could have passed by. There are millions of other books you could be reading right now. For whatever reason, the Spirit put this page before your eyes. Why? Perhaps, just perhaps, the Lord wants some face-to-face, soul-to-soul contact with you in this moment. He's saying: "You know what? Give Me something to drink. I'm thirsty for your soul. I'm more thirsty for your salvation than you are; I'm more thirsty for you to know Me than you are. Are you willing to give Me something to drink? Are you willing to lose the facade? Are you ready to let Me love you?"

If you're in that place where you constantly feel as if you're being pulled back to the past, it's not time to walk to confession, *it's time to run* — to experience the love of the Father that can never go away and never be lost.

It's fascinating that in this conversation in Samaria the woman says that she sees Jesus is "a prophet," and a little later refers to Him as "the Christ." By the end of the encounter she believes He is the Savior. A prophet might know what others don't know, an anointed heart might speak with piercing truth, but only the Savior can save. She leaves that jar of water and goes back to the town where they gossip about her and judge her, but now she is completely free, a new missionary. She goes back and shares the love of Christ with those who have not been good to her. The woman is unafraid and unashamed because God has given her the gift she so desperately needed.

A Step Beyond

How often do you take advantage of the Sacrament of Reconciliation? Are you frequenting the sacrament? If not, why not? The more grace is overflowing from you, the more others will be drawn to it themselves. Go back to the well! While there, see, too, what happened after one sinner sipped from the chalice of God's mercy. The truth of the Samaritan woman's newfound freedom was, then, shared with even more souls who came to believe:

> **Many** Samaritans from that city **believed in him because of the woman's testimony**, "He told me all that I ever did." So when the Samaritans came to him, they asked him to stay with them; and he stayed there two days. And many more believed because of his word. They said to the woman, "**It is no longer because of your words that we believe, for we have heard for ourselves, and we know that this is indeed the Savior of the world.**" (John 4:39-42, emphasis added)

This woman's words — her personal witness — led countless others to seek Christ on their own. Her humility bore witness and invited former enemies into a relationship with God. Her words did not invite them into her personal relationship with Christ as much as they invited people to seek Christ on their own!

People with no realization of sin still need the Savior. Sin is death. Christ is life.

And, He is seeking you.

Now be honest with yourself. Are you hiding from Him? Have you taken to seeking the sin over the Savior? Have you fallen into the trap of holding your breath in the darkness, silent and motionless, rather than penitent and prayerful?

He loves us even more than we love ourselves. That's a fact (see 1 Jn 4). He's also coming back at some point; that's also a fact (see, well, the New Testament). That fact is only "scary" if we're not where we need to be in relationship to God. A relationship with Jesus is all the fun without any of the games. Expose your soul before God and allow Him to love you for who you truly are: a sinner in need of His mercy, an unrefined but glorious work in progress.

As hide-and-seek reminds us: "Ready or not … here He comes."

Chapter 3

Encountering Jesus Unveils Your True Vocation

Christ and Simon (Peter)

Frustration set in. Their hands bleeding, their forearms sore, and their blood pressure assuredly rising. The boat revealed empty nets. For a husband and father, the emptiness must have struck a deeper level — an entire night with nothing to show for it. Nights like these weren't good news for a family. As a fisherman, you can rely only so much on hard work and skill; at some point, creation (more pointedly, the Creator) needs to provide if your fishing business is to stay "afloat." Simon had obviously enjoyed success in his fishing trade with his brother, Andrew. They had the Zebedee family as partners, multiple ships (see Lk 5:7) and crew cost money ... you don't get to that level by scraping by each day.

Imagine the pressure of feeding your family and simultaneously lining the money purses of the Romans. (And, by extension, their duplicitous Israelite tax collectors, such as Matthew.) How stressful the fishless haul must have been, compounded by daybreak, working your fingers to the bone — sometimes, literally — repeatedly casting and pulling the nets with nothing to show for it but sweat and growing frustration.

Then up walks the itinerant carpenter from Nazareth, long on enigmatic charisma but short on practical angling, and by the looks of Jesus, He obviously didn't strike the professional fisherman as an expert.

Baiting the fishermen

The Holy Spirit offers us the scene through St. Luke's mighty pen:

> While the people pressed upon him [Jesus] … he saw two boats by the lake…. Getting into one of the boats, which was Simon's, he asked him to put out a little from the land…. When he had ceased speaking, he said to Simon, "Put out into the deep and let down your nets for a catch." And Simon answered, "Master, we toiled all night and took nothing! But at your word I will let down the nets." And when they had done this, they enclosed a great shoal of fish; and … their nets were breaking…. When Simon Peter saw it, he fell down at Jesus' knees, saying, "Depart from me, for I am a sinful man, O Lord." (Luke 5:1-8)

Consider the supposed gall of Christ in this scene. These are professional fishermen who tackle the unpredictable storms of Galilee at every turn. These are sailors, most likely with attitudes, tempers, and possibly even sailor language to boot. Make no mistake, Galilee's sons were far from choirboys — they were men on every level, tradesmen by day, rebels by night, living under the painful and oppressive yoke of Rome season after season, catch after catch. This is the group — broken, prideful, and tired — to whom the Lord not only draws near but bids to head back out on the water after the literal all-nighter.

Simon (Peter)'s response offers more than a glimpse into the soul of our first pope. This was not a kindly or affable retort to an unreasonable request. The tone we witness from the future leader of the apostolic Church is downright annoyed, and borderline condescending: "We've been at this all night, Mr. Carpenter … and you want to tell the sailors how it's done, huh?" You can almost hear the indignation in his voice. Still, what made him push off from shore again? Do you ever ask yourself that?

Our God is not lacking in creative solutions to ordinary issues.

Was it something in Jesus's tone that left Simon (Peter) intrigued? Was it something in the Lord's glance that led Simon to move those tired and exhausted arms toward the oars and sail, once again? What does it take to move a weary soul into uncharted — and therefore, dangerous — waters? What happens when God calls *us* out into the deep? Do we rebuff Him? Yes, frequently. Do we lodge our complaint, so it's "on record"? Yes, often. Do we follow God loyally but unwillingly (out of fear of consequence)? More often than we'd like to admit, probably. And does God consistently surpass, bless, shatter, and rebuild our myopic and self-centered expectations? Absolutely, He does. Our God is not lacking in creative solutions to ordinary issues. He knows what we'll say before we even pray it, yet He listens, validates, and, then invites us "into the deep," to rechannel our issues into effort and, in the process, gain the most valuable of all pearls ... that of perspective. We must never forget that not only some things, but ALL things, are possible in Christ (see Phil 4:13; Mk 9:23).

Just a fish story?

When is the last time you rolled your eyes at God? Think about it. You felt led to leave your job but didn't have anything else lined up. You had to deal with "*that* family member" but saw it more as a burden than an opportunity. You were serving at your church but felt unsupported, unnoticed, or unappreciated. You got a call, email, or text that left you feeling persecuted, abandoned, or alone ... when you "knew" God was there but sure didn't feel it. *Hello, Simon, welcome to the shore of Galilee.*

While sacred Scripture is clear about at least two storms on the Sea of Galilee during Christ's earthly missionary journey (see Mk 4:35-41 and Mt 14:22-33), I believe and would argue that the first account of a storm on Galilee's waters actually took place on a docked boat, on the sea of Simon Peter's heart. He had doubted God's power, providence, and plan. He, like you and I, tried to make God fit into His plans rather than vice versa ... and that never, ever ends well.

The storm clouds circled, I imagine, as the fish began to leap into the tearing nets that morning. The fisherman attempted to correct the carpenter. What began as a lesson in angling ended as a lesson on angle-ing, where the divine shed light on humanity from an entirely new angle. Maybe, just maybe, God was not distant but near; was it possible that the woodworker knew more about the spiritual location of the fisherman than even the physical location of the fish?

On his knees, through clenched fists and tear-drenched eyes, a hailstorm of self-awareness rushed upon Simon (Peter). His ego crushed, his pride rent, and his weakness revealed. His newfound awareness of his own unworthiness in the presence of God caused him to bid the Lord go, but peering into the eyes of Divine Mercy left the future saint unwilling to let go. How could this miracle worker, this "Rabbi," have known the hiding spot for the fish or their fisherman? "Depart from me," Simon bids, but the Lord had no such intention (see *Catechsim of the Catholic Church*, 208; also Is 6:5; Gn 18:27).

The Lord isn't content with us wading in the shallow end of the spiritual pool.

I believe Simon's reaction is our first inclination, as well, when, as sinners, we push God away when He gets "too intimate" or too close. *Souls trapped in darkness just cannot handle the jolting presence of such pure Light.* So we keep Him at bay, anchor Him in the cove of the intellectual. It's when we realize that God's love is unconditional, though, and His mercy unwavering, that our heart and head are freed from the lies of sin and empowered to step out in grace.

Hook, line, and sinker

No wonder they left their nets that day: How could anything compare to what (and whom) they had found? Little did they know that that initial following of Christ, that first conversion, would be the easiest step of their newfound life in Christ. It's a lesson every believer must learn on their own, that the initial surrender to Jesus, though scary, is in retrospect the easiest of all that follow. The Lord, as we see here, isn't content with us wading in the shallow end of the spiritual pool. God will always call us into the deep, for it's where we experience His glory and discover our true vocation.

Now, fast-forward beyond that emotional, first storm in Simon's heart to the next storm we read about in Scripture, where God is sleeping (see Mk 4:38) or, worse yet, not even in the boat (Mt 14:23-33), only showing up dramatically, after hours of torturous waves and loss of hope.

You've felt it before as I have. You're in the thick of it — things are unraveling; the outlook is bleak and peace is lacking. You feel like God is sleeping or, at the very least, simply doesn't really care. You pray … and nothing. You cry out and, again, nada. You kneel, you scream, you beseech, you despair … and nothing but silence.

God is nowhere. Stare deeply into that sentence for a minute. Those three words usher in a hopeless reality, a world of despair, and a reality that too many in the world sadly believe.

But what if we created some space for God within our hearts? What if we, like Simon (Peter), heard the voice of the Nazarene carpenter and, out of nothing less than sheer intrigue, gave Him "a chance" at our soul? What if you, after lodging your issues, complaints, and doubts, pushed back out into the deep, again? What if you and I allowed the seemingly silent God "who must not love me" to take us by the hand again? We would be wise to believe the promise God gave us through the mighty prophet Isaiah:

> "I have chosen you and not cast you off"; / fear not, for I am with you, / be not dismayed, for I am your God; / I will strengthen you, I will help you, / I will uphold you with my victorious right hand. (Isaiah 41:9-10)

If I could tattoo a verse on my brain, this would be it, a constant reminder that God never abandons me but that I frequently abandon Him. I need a consistent and continual visible reminder that it's not me pursuing God, but instead God pursuing me! He is the Good Shepherd, traversing valleys and mountains and riverbeds, shouting out to this lost sheep, wandering in the valleys of torment, sin, and self-centeredness. His call evokes an urge in me to return but often leaves me feeling as if I've strayed too far from the shepherd's protection or the master's forgiveness. These are pure lies, because no distance, no sin, no selfishness can separate us; unless St. Paul is a liar:

> If God is for us, who is against us? He who did not spare his own Son but gave him up for us all, will he not also give us all things with him? Who shall bring any charge against God's elect? It is God who justifies; who is to condemn? Is it Christ Jesus, who died, yes, who was raised from the dead, who is at the right hand of God, who indeed intercedes for us? Who shall separate us from the love of Christ? Shall tribulation, or distress, or persecution, or famine, or nakedness, or peril, or sword? (Romans 8:31-35)

So what happens if we create that space in our hearts for God's life that we call "grace"? What happens if we pray and repent and — best of all — run to the Father's embrace in confession, again? That little space transforms hopelessness to hope, a premise to a promise. Consider what a difference a little space makes ... **God is now here.**

Mercy doesn't need a valley or a gorge; it occupies even that smallest crevice in the sin-tattered heart and life-fatigued soul. All God needs to forgive you is the invitation, and we can extend it at any time. God's mercy is waiting, a mere prayer away at any time, day or night. Mercy is free — offered even before we ask — but the action is expensive; mercy comes only after we lay down our invaluable crown (pride) at the feet of our true Lord.

Stop and reflect now: When have you rolled your eyes at God because your plan was better? When have you been exasperated by life because His response came "too slowly"? When were you most aware of your own sinfulness or struggled to trust that you were worthy of the mercy God wished to offer you?

Why not now? Why not ask the Lord to trample on the waves of your heart, again? Galilee is not as far as you think. No, most days your Sea of Galilee is your neighborhood parish and Christ is bidding you to go *deeper*. Note what Jesus invites them to do, *after they've already been at it* ***their way*** *all night*. Get in the boat. Lift the anchor. Pick up those nets with your tired hands. Keep your grumblings to yourself. Get to work, but do so empowered by God's life that we call *grace*. When the mission is His and not ours, the nonstop work becomes constant privilege.

> *All God needs to forgive you is the invitation, and we can extend it at any time.*

Have you yet accepted God's invitation to confession (we spoke about this in the last chapter), where Christ calls you out of your comfort zone in the midst of life's sins and storms, to rescue you from your world, your sin, and, in many cases, your*self*? Sometimes an invitation must be offered multiple times before a heart relents. Sometimes the Spirit uses others to give us that nudge toward the grace we so desperately need.

Mercy breathes in the most unexpected of places, such as upon a cross in the midst of crucifixion, and in every confessional for two thousand years since.

A Step Beyond

Before we can really serve God, or even know God, we must come face to face — as Simon Peter did — with who we are and, more importantly, who we are not. Before we can "catch others" in God's net, we must slow down and allow ourselves to be caught.

Christ is calling you to something more, something far greater than perhaps you have even realized thus far in your life. If you want to experience the greatest joy this life has to offer, it begins with discerning what God created you for and whether or not you are currently fulfilling your mission here on earth.

While the call to follow Jesus may appear exciting and inspiring at first glance, time reveals that the romanticism quickly fades as we learn that serving God means you'll be asked to give everything you have … and then some.

Still want in? Still willing to put out into the deep of Christ, that you may be "caught"? When we put our lives into His hands we are never left empty-handed. In fact, we're often left with far more than we bargained for.

Chapter 4

Encountering Jesus Magnifies Your Gifts

Christ and "Eddie"

At age ten, I decided I wanted to make some money. My allowance just wasn't cutting it. There were skateboard parts to buy and video games to master, so I told my parents I needed a raise in my meager allowance.

Like good parents (of six kids), they told me to get a job.

Challenge accepted. Over the next few years, I delivered thousands of newspapers. I delivered more than two hundred papers a day, in fact. Long before people got their news online, I was their search engine. I had a spotless record and a growing bank account, and I took pride in my work. Once high school started, though, I had to find a different job, one that worked with my schedules for school, sports, and other activities. I had tasted freedom with my own stream of income, and I didn't want to live without it. I soon traded in newspapers for a spot-ridden apron and tray. I took a job as a lowly busboy in a nearby restaurant.

I never understood why they called the job "busboy." Later, though, I learned that the word "busboy" comes from the Latin word *omnibus*, which means "for all." It applies to busboys because it is their job to do "anything and everything for anyone and everyone" in the restaurant. Truthfully, that was both a prophetic and appropriate designation.

I did do everything. I set tables, delivered food (when servers were lazy or distracted), cleared plates, restocked sundries, wiped down tables, swept, and vacuumed. You name it, and I did it. Customers didn't know my name, nor did they seem to care. No one outside of God and my guardian angel actually knew how hard I was working behind the scenes or how badly I needed money, either, especially since I was saving for college. The only things that mattered to the customers was that their water glasses were always full, their baskets of chips were abundant, and the salsa endlessly flowed like a waterfall of spicy goodness. I was on the main stage every night, but somehow I remained almost anonymous and behind the scenes. When people left that restaurant overly hydrated, more stuffed than the enchiladas, and gassier than an eighteen-wheeler, I knew my work there was done. Sure, each night the waiters may have left with more money in their pockets, but I fell into bed with the great satisfaction of knowing I had gone above and beyond the call of duty.

Note how God miraculously responded to the needs of the many through the surrendered gift of the one.

Tradition tells us that the great St. Martha (of Bethany), sister to Mary and Lazarus, is the patron saint of waiters and waitresses. You might remember how she waited on and served the Lord (see Lk 10:38-42) while her sister sat at His feet. St. Martha may own that patronage for food servers, but, technically, there is no official patron saint designated specifically for busboys or busgirls, but if there were, I know what Gospel character I'd nominate!

Jesus and the lunch rush

Scripture tells us (and Tradition and historians affirm) that Jesus performed countless miracles during His time on earth. We are beyond blessed that many of them were recorded for us in the Gospels. In fact, beyond the Resurrection, the multiplication of loaves and fish is the only miracle that appears in all four Gospel accounts. Consider that fact for a moment, because it's worthy of a second and third thought.

You have probably heard this story more times than you can count. We hear it, annually, at Mass and on specific holy days. But, sometimes, it's important to read it again, with your own eyes. It's easy for stories we've heard often to appear to be just that — stories, rather than life-changing and soul-altering truths. Don't let the biblical passage that follows become merely words upon a page. Pause and pray before you read the Words of God that follow; in doing so you'll undoubtedly pick up on little details you might have missed in the past:

> After this Jesus went to the other side of the Sea of Galilee, which is the Sea of Tiberias. And a multitude followed him, because they saw the signs which he did on those who were diseased. Jesus went up on the mountain, and there sat down with his disciples. Now the Passover, the feast of the Jews, was at hand. Lifting up his eyes, then, and seeing that a multitude was coming to him, Jesus said to Philip, "How are we to buy bread, so that these people may eat?" This he said to test him, for he himself knew what he would do. Philip answered him, "Two hundred denarii

> would not buy enough bread for each of them to get a little." One of his disciples, Andrew, Simon Peter's brother, said to him, "There is a lad here who has five barley loaves and two fish; but what are they among so many?" Jesus said, "Make the people sit down." Now there was much grass in the place; so the men sat down, in number about five thousand. Jesus then took the loaves, and when he had given thanks, he distributed them to those who were seated; so also the fish, as much as they wanted. And when they had eaten their fill, he told his disciples, "Gather up the fragments left over, that nothing may be lost." So they gathered them up and filled twelve baskets with fragments from the five barley loaves, left by those who had eaten. When the people saw the sign which he had done, they said, "This is indeed the prophet who is to come into the world!" (John 6:1-14)

There is so much happening in this passage. It's easy to lose some of the meat — or fish, as it were — of the story amidst the details. Work through the following questions to see how closely you paid attention to the details. In doing so, we begin to learn about ourselves, how we approach Scripture, and what types of details tend to "jump out" at us:

- Where did this miracle take place? Next to what famous site?
- When did this take place? During what feast?
- How much money would still not be enough to feed everyone?
- Who tells Jesus about the boy with the food?
- How much food does the boy have?

- What kind of bread was it?
- How many men were there, not counting the women and children?
- What, specifically, did Jesus do with the bread and fish?
- How much food was left over after Jesus's miracle?
- Did you catch any details you had forgotten?

Did you notice anything new in the story? Do you see how the Lord is interacting with His Church through His apostles? Note how God miraculously responded to the needs of the many through the surrendered gift of the one. Often in Scripture, as in life, we don't retain or even notice what God is doing because we're not paying attention to the details in our life. It's easy to question or even blame God for our physical or spiritual hunger when, in reality, He was providing — if we had eyes to see it and a heart humble enough to believe it. Sometimes, however, it takes letting a situation play out fully before we see the fruit that the personal sacrifice bore.

Almost famous

Now, over the years, I've heard a lot of priests and speakers preach about "the boy with the loaves and the fish." They always praised his generosity and affirmed his sacrifice. It was a noble and benevolent act on the part of the young lad in Galilee that day, to be sure. And while I don't want to disagree, because the boy does deserve our admiration, these homilies and talks always annoy me a little.

First, I have never liked the fact that this kid didn't have a name. I mean, of course he had a name, but the Gospel writers don't tell us what it is, which bothers me. Why did the Holy Spirit omit or "fail to inspire" the Evangelists to include such a fact?

I mean, if this kid is so important, why didn't someone stop to get a name? Why didn't St. Matthew ask the young whippersnapper for his surname, so as to properly cite it later? Perhaps the Lord may have wanted to send a thank-you note for the boy's assist that day when the hungry masses were pressing in. I've thought a lot about this scene, and I'd like to respectfully submit that we call this famous young boy Eddie. Think about it. Eddie sounds like a good guy. Eddie's the kind of kid who will share his lunch with you at school when you accidentally leave yours on the counter at home. Yep, I vote that from here on out, or at least in this book, we officially refer to "the loaves and fish kid" as good ol' Eddie.

Next, while I like Eddie, and certainly appreciate his go-getter attitude and penchant for being in the right place at the right time, let's not be so quick to heap lauds upon him. Why must every speaker paint such a heroic picture of Eddie, anyway? We praise this boy because he turned over his lunch to a bunch of hungry-looking, grown men. I mean, think about it for a second. If you're a young guy and some big dudes (sailors, no less) surround you and ask, "Hey kid, what's in your basket?" then you have two choices: one results in a potential pummeling by men short on patience and long on hunger, and the other results in an unintentional fast for the remainder of the day. I sometimes wonder if Eddie may not have been as courageous as he was just plain smart!

While we obviously have no way of knowing the truth, it is fun to think about, isn't it? Scripture should capture our imagination and cause us to think. It should be entertaining and enjoyable, not just informative; our encounters with the Word of God ought to be *transformative* because Christ himself is the living Word of God. We must immerse ourselves in the story as we might immerse ourselves in the deep end of the swimming pool. When you're reading a story, don't just ask, "What is this saying to me?" Really put yourself into the scene, into each character's sandals, and ask, "What is this saying about me?"

The one who serves

Take in the scene. Picture the throngs of people. Envision the anonymous boy scurrying along the shoreline. Feel the dampness of the humidity in the air during the spring month as Passover loomed. Take in the aroma of fish and the stench of the hungry, unwashed masses pressing in. Hear the apostles' discourse as they frantically sought a solution to the people's problem. This was an emotionally charged moment, to be sure.

Now, consider yourself when you are hungry. How patient are you? How reasonable? Picture yourself when others' problems become your own, the sense of ownership you take on as you go into problem-solving mode. Next, turn your attention to a humble-hearted young boy caught between Simon Peter and the hungry masses — he was, quite literally, between "the Rock" and a hard place.

Picture Eddie's face as his miniscule offering was brought to the Master. It's hard to imagine he didn't follow the food in hopes of at least a tiny return on his unexpected investment. This biblical busboy would have assuredly wanted to see a profit from this mighty Nazarene prophet. Imagine his eyes as he looked into the Master's. Visualize the amazement at seeing all that was created from such a humble offering.

Eddie didn't set out to be a hero. We don't even know what he was doing there that day. Maybe he just noticed the crowd while walking by the Sea of Galilee and decided to investigate. Maybe, like a teenager named David long before him, he was just delivering lunch to someone in his family when he found himself in an awkward situation. David took on a giant warrior with five smooth stones; Eddie took on a giant hunger with five barley loaves. Even more remarkable is that barley was considered "poor people's food" and the "loaves" were likely more the size of small buns or rolls. Since the boy was apparently not wealthy, his sacrifice becomes that much more meaningful, as Our Lord reminded us when the widow gave her final two coins as alms for the "poor" (Lk 21:2).

Virtue doesn't begin with a desire to be heroic, though, it begins with a desire to get better.

Not coincidentally, immediately following Jesus's miracle with the loaves and fish, He goes for a walk on water. In fact, it's then and only then that He explains in great detail an even greater truth and forthcoming miracle involving both the bread and His body: the "bread of life" discourse gives us the foundational understanding for the holy Eucharist (see Jn 6:22-71). While we can't treat this great Catholic gift — the source and summit of our faith — expansively or in detail here, suffice to say it was only after Our Lord demonstrated His power over the gifts of creation (loaves and fish) and revealed His power over His own body and the elements (walking upon the water) that He *then* opens our minds and enraptures our souls with the truth of the forthcoming Eucharistic grace.

And little Eddie had a front pew seat for all of it … just as we do at *every single Mass*. The Gospel of Luke reminds us that Jesus received sinners and ate with them (see 15:1). *He still does* this at every Catholic Mass. You may not find it heroic to go to Mass. You may not even know what you are doing there half the time, or why you may have stopped going at some point out of guilt or shame. Virtue doesn't begin with a desire to be heroic, though. It begins with a desire to get better.

A return on your investment

Possibly, the most important part of Eddie's story isn't what he did, but why he did it. What did he hear in the apostles' voices? I may have joked that he gave what little he had out of fear of consequence (and, to be sure, some still do have that as the impetus for their generosity to those less fortunate). I feel strongly, though, that it was something far deeper within the young man that was unleashed. The voice of Christ and the needs of His church moved a young and humble heart to serve. What did he see in God's eyes? The youngster was most likely from a poor family. He probably fit right in with the masses of people who came to Jesus hungry. Only this day, for some reason, Eddie had some food. He didn't know what Christ was going to do, but he gave the Lord what little, yet all, that he had. That fateful day beside the Sea of Galilee, earth looked to heaven, creation to its Creator, and Love not only fulfilled expectations, He far exceeded them. Christ honored Eddie's humble sacrifice, blessing thousands of people in the (sacramental) process. Sound familiar?

All Eddie did was give back to God what he had already been given. That food, while it was technically Eddie's, was really God's. Every gift you have is a gift from God. Everything you have, even those things you buy with your own money, is a gift from God, for our very ability to earn money is a God-given grace.

Eddie didn't withhold creation (loaves and fish) from his Creator and, as a result, even more of God's creation (literally thousands) was blessed by it. Never underestimate how much God can do with a little. Never underestimate how much God can do with you, an ordinary person, on an ordinary day.

Eddie's example inspires me, and it ought to challenge all of us to ask difficult questions about how we really "surrender" to God on a daily basis:

- Have you ever given ***everything*** you had to the Lord?
- Do you give your absolute *best* in everything you do?
- Is it more desirable for you to be famous or to be faithful?
- Would you rather be rich or holy?
- Do you think Eddie would care that his name isn't listed in the Gospel accounts?

Eddie witnessed a miracle of love. He witnessed God in action. The God of the universe thought enough of Eddie to invite him to play a vital role in one of the most famous and miraculous moments in history. The boy looked Love in the eyes and watched how Love magnified his little act of love. Eddie's life was instantly changed forever. The ironic part, too, is that while Eddie gave it all to God, he *lost* nothing. Eddie, too, alongside the throngs of people, ended that day with a very full stomach. He probably even got to take leftovers home if he had a to-go container (as any good busboy would).

Have you ever felt as if you had to be known, or rich, or famous before you could bless the Lord, build His kingdom, or do something of consequence?

You don't. Eddie knows it. God knows it. Sometimes we put God on hold or on pause until we feel as if we have more influence. We don't speak up until we "grow up." We don't offer anything until we think we have something more substantial to offer. There we go … thinking like sheep rather than the Shepherd. God didn't measure Eddie's worth on the size of the tithe, only on the heart behind it. It's not about the size of the gift; it's about the motivation behind itto. Just think about how many people benefited from Eddie's charity, and not just the thousands on the shore of the sea. *Billions* of souls have read and heard this true story, having their lives both challenged and blessed by it.

For a nameless kid, he made quite a name for himself. How about you?

Do you worry that your best just isn't good enough? You have more to offer than you think. When you give God your everything, He can do amazing, miraculous things.

The first thing you have to do is remember where your gifts, talents, and blessings come from. They are all gifts from God. When you put them back into His hands, for His use and for His glory, He can (and will) do incredible things — not only in your life, but also in the countless lives of other people. You are powerful beyond your wildest dreams. Did you know that? There is power in sacrifice. And, just as Jesus did with Eddie, God not only unleashes that power when you put your gifts into His hands, He multiplies those gifts!

Pour your best into everything you do. Take pride in your work. Whatever it is that you are called to do and whatever you like to do, hold nothing back. Do it supremely well. Give it your best, because the God who gave you your blessings and talents deserves your best at all times (see Col 3:15-17).

You don't have to be all things to all people, but you're invited to be the absolute best version of yourself that you can be, every hour of the day. And you can do that by putting others first, by serving them just as Jesus did (see Jn 13:15). If you live this way, you won't be bussing the banquet table in heaven. You'll be sitting as the guest of honor, right beside Jesus, enjoying the fruits of a job well done and a life well lived.

A Step Beyond

What gifts do you have to offer? What skills and talents did God entrust to you? Now, how are you using them to build the kingdom of heaven on earth and not just make your earthly kingdom feel more "heavenly"?

Are you currently serving at your parish? How about in other ministries? How are you putting your gifts and talents at the service of the Lord (see 1 Pt 4:10)? Are you giving all you have and doing all you can to be part of the solution to the Church's problems? Do you grab a basin and towel and offer to wash feet, or just sit idly by pointing out how bad the feet smell?

Hop to it, Eddie … the people of God are hungry and His table needs to be set when people come looking for His heavenly food!

Chapter 5

Encountering Jesus Calls You into a Relationship

Christ and the Rich Young Man

Is there urgency to your prayer life?

If I were to offer you one dollar would it be worth the twenty seconds it would take you to email me your home address? Would you accept the offer and do so? Would you take the time to respond for such a minimal amount of money?

What if I offered you fifty dollars — no strings attached — to email me your mailing address? Again, if you knew me, knew I was not scamming you, and that it was completely out of the kindness of my *obviously* benevolent heart ... would you do it?

What if I offered you one thousand dollars? Would that be enough of an incentive for you to write me back? Now, what if I offered you fifty thousand or one hundred thousand dollars?

What if I offered you one million dollars if you only had to email me your mailing address?

For anyone reading this who trusted in the offer and believed it to be legit, the number of people who'd actually write in would undoubtedly grow as the worth of the prize grew. It's basic human logic. The urgency we assign to something is directly proportional to the value we place upon it.

Now, apply that same principle to your daily prayer life, to confession, or to the holy Mass. How much time and effort do you put into your prayer life and your faith walk? If prayer and, by extension, our relationship with God is primary in our life, then it will naturally show in the urgency and primacy we place upon it.

This exercise isn't intended to make any of us feel bad. We can all improve our prayer lives. It is designed to help us take a realistic inventory of the role prayer does (or ought to) play in our lives. Make no mistake: prayer does not merely "help" our relationship with God … prayer *is our relationship with God.*

If you're going to live the Christian life, your peace and ultimate joy will be directly correlated to how strong your prayer life is and continues to become. Prayer isn't optional. Your faith journey is beset on all sides by the lies and lures of our painfully self-focused modern culture. If you are seeking God, the devil is seeking you (see Rom 7:21). The future saints of our Church (our kids and grandkids) need saints-in-training (you and me) to be their mentors on this moral battlefield they're making their way through.

In accepting this challenge, you are accepting God's battle plan for their (and your) salvation, and that battle plan requires great discipline and sacrifice on your part. The question is not, How strong is your prayer life currently? but, rather, How strongly are you dedicated to making your daily prayer life better? How far are you willing to go? What are you willing to sacrifice, to "lose," that those souls you love most don't lose that which is most important?

If we want our relationship with God to become its strongest, we must allow the Holy Spirit to begin with the areas that are weakest.

If you want to see where your heart really is, pay attention to where your mind goes when it wanders. The truth that Christ gave us in the Gospel of Matthew is as poignant, practical, and timeless as anything else in the Gospels:

> "For where your treasure is, there will your heart be also." (6:21)

This passage pierces souls just as directly in the twenty-first century as it did in the first. Commit this verse to memory and make the commitment, today, to identify the areas of your life most in need of spiritual fine-tuning or overhaul, and invite the Holy Spirit to go to work on you.

It's easy to move through life reactively, offering back to God only that which we are comfortable letting go of, but when we do, what have we really achieved? Anyone can give out of excess. No, Christ isn't nearly as interested in what we are currently "doing" in the name of our faith as much as He desires that which we refuse to surrender. The God who would mount the cross — and bid us to carry our own — repeatedly went above and beyond, and challenged us to do the same.

Let's consider one of the most famous interactions in the Gospel narrative, when the pious, rich young lad went looking for heaven, only to be brought crashing down to earth.

All of this … and *then some*

> And behold, one came up to him, saying, "Teacher, what good deed must I do, to have eternal life?" And

> he said to him, "Why do you ask me about what is good? One there is who is good. If you would enter life, keep the commandments." He said to him, "Which?" And Jesus said, "You shall not kill, You shall not commit adultery, You shall not steal, You shall not bear false witness, Honor your father and mother, and, You shall love your neighbor as yourself." The young man said to him, "All these I have observed; what do I still lack?" Jesus said to him, "If you would be perfect, go, sell what you possess and give to the poor, and you will have treasure in heaven; and come, follow me." When the young man heard this he went away sorrowful; for he had great possessions....
>
> But many that are first will be last, and the last first. (Matthew 19:16-30)

There Jesus goes again being "illogical." We may ask: The last shall be first, Jesus? In what free-market economy is that the reality? What economic model are you suggesting, and how is it scalable on the global stage? In what sports league, competition, or race is coming in last preferable? Who remembers the loser? How can donating my assets get me ahead on any social scale? I mean, has Jesus ever taken an economics class or workshop on leadership?

Why would God offer freedom and salvation to the person who surrendered that which enabled them to help others? Why would God tell us this path to perfection would come only through total self-sacrifice? Easy for God's kid to say such things, right? He didn't have a family to feed or a mortgage to pay. The Son of Man had no place to lay his head (see Mt 8:20); the itinerant carpenter-turned-preacher didn't have monthly bills to cover. And why the stern tone with the young upstart so passionately following the moral law and so desiring to go deeper in his faith? Shouldn't this young man have been praised rather than scolded? I mean, at least this kid *was trying*! Does God not see the countless masses who don't give a flying anything when it comes to faith and God and religion?

In short, why was Jesus calling the young man on the proverbial carpet? Didn't the fishers of men have far larger fish to fry?

Before we get to the meat of the verse, I find it helpful to envision Christ's glance in this episode. Perhaps read the words above again, and try to hear Christ's tone and inflection as He speaks to the passionate young truth seeker.

The urgency we assign to something is directly proportional to the value we place upon it.

Does Jesus really sound upset to you? Or is it something more? I believe He senses a genuine passion and desire in the young man. Perhaps Jesus, then, uses this moment to redirect and unleash the fullness of said passion. Is the Lord just trying to teach *all of us* worldly souls about how deadly numbing this world can be? Is Christ inviting us to a life of material servitude or spiritual freedom?

The Lord is revealing to us that a relationship with Him extends far beyond compliance. In all reality, the heavenly Father is revealing that His most ardent, most deep-seated desire for us is rooted in relationship and not merely in ritual or rule. What begins with a response of intrigue actually culminates in a call to intimacy.

This is not the "rich young man versus God," but more to the point, God "versing" the rich young man. Perhaps we would glean more of the depth of this simple exchange taking it line by line or verse by verse, as it were:

> And behold, one came up to him, saying, "Teacher, what good deed must I do, to have eternal life?" (Matthew 19:16)

Note that it was the young man who sought Jesus in this instance, not the other way around. The young man was proactively seeking truth, and Truth Incarnate responded. As we have already seen, when we go seeking, God does not hide from us (see Jer 29:12), not if we have the eyes of faith (Mt 13:15-16). Notice, too, that the young man addresses Christ not yet as Savior or even healer but as Teacher. Unaware of the depth and breadth of Jesus's identity, the youth views faith through the lens of an external reality — a set of dos and don'ts — rather than an internal posture that illuminates and animates his faith into action. Put simply, the cart was missing the horse.

> And he said to him, "Why do you ask me about what is good? One there is who is good." (Matthew 19:17a)

With this seemingly odd retort to modern minds, Jesus employs a Platonic approach to a conversation, initiating a deeper dialogue by positing a question in response to his original interrogative statement. In the Greek equivalent of a mental chess match, the small-town carpenter demonstrates big-city wit and gives us a glimpse into the Father's heart. God *is good*, and in recognizing Jesus as "good" the young man is plunged deeper into the reality few until now have fully come to grasp.

> "If you would enter life, keep the commandments." He said to him, "Which?" And Jesus said, "You shall not kill, You shall not commit adultery, You shall not steal, You shall not bear false witness, Honor your fa-

> ther and mother, and, You shall love your neighbor as yourself." (vv. 17b-19)

Can merely keeping the commandments ensure that you or I will get to heaven? Assuredly, a strict obedience to God's precepts will not hurt our chances of salvation, but it extends far deeper, does it not? A healthy diet may battle a life-threatening disease, but it cannot rightly conquer it. A strict exercise regimen might help keep us healthy but does little after we are already deathly ill. The letter of the law can do only so much for us if we do not first adhere to the spirit of it. In time, laws fade and obedience falters if our hearts are more concerned about the "what" than the One who gave it to us. The rich young man may have never broken the speed limit, but he had no idea why he was driving or how much fuel it would take to get where he was going. He had the directions, but his spiritual tank was on fumes, and Jesus knew it. The young man could do no more on his own. Proudly, he offered:

> "All these I have observed; what do I still lack?" (v. 20)

How fascinating and truthfully humble: this young man, so obedient and seemingly holy, recognized that he was lacking something. What a gut check for us modern readers who so often judge our own holiness by our lack of friends and neighbors.

How often do we go to the Lord, keenly aware of our own (almost beloved) sins … fully compliant in leaving the doors of sin and addiction open in our own lives, but so quick to point out the flaws and misgivings of other, far more "sinful" souls. Thank God for sunglasses, which make it so much easier to hide our corneal logs as we focus on others' splinters (see Mt 7:1-5). How daunting, too, is Jesus's response to this man whose holiness in action would put many of us to shame?

> Jesus said to him, "If you would be perfect, go, sell what you possess and give to the poor, and you will have treasure in heaven; and come, follow me." (v. 21)

Let's be clear: this is not Jesus asking a middle-income earner to tithe a little more on Sundays. This is the God of the universe telling a rich man to give away *everything* and follow Him and Him alone. This is not only an invitation, it is a command, a challenge, and I would submit a divinely inspired secret to life: if you want it all, give it all. We cannot receive heaven if we are constantly clutching earth.

The lesson goes back to Eden, when our ancestors in faith grasped earth, forsaking heaven. But Christ "not count[ing] equality with God something to be ***grasped***, but emptied himself, took the form of a servant [slave], being born in the likeness of men" (Phil 2:6-7, emphasis added).

It is in letting it all go that we actually receive it all. Life is death (to self) and death is gain (see Phil 1:21). It is not only in the giving that we receive, but it is in the action of giving all of ourselves, in our self-gift to others, that we finally discover our true selves (Rom 12:1).

A gift is just an intention until it is offered and received by another.

Possibly the most striking line in the passage, though, is seemingly the most simple. Did you notice that Jesus instructed the rich man to give everything *to the poor*? It seems like common sense, right? Of course he'd give it to the poor. Who needs it more? But consider what this does to the social structure and status of the rich man, currently "above" the poor. In giving all his possessions to those "beneath" him, the rich man now relegates himself to their care.

He now places himself beneath those currently under him. The one who scaled the corporate ladder would now have not a single rung to stand on. His dependence would now fall squarely on the former have-nots and the homeless preacher. This call to put up or shut up proved too much for the young man, and, I would submit, it is still too daunting for most of us in the modern age. Is his response one of self-gift or self-preservation? Was he willing to go above and beyond? Am I? Are you? These are the questions that ought to smack us in the face with every turn of sacred Scripture's page.

We cannot receive heaven if we are constantly clutching earth.

> When the young man heard this he went away sorrowful; for he had great possessions. But many that are first will be last, and the last first." (vv. 16,30)

Everlasting life, the invitation to the eternal and deepest possible intimacy with God comes at a cost. Our salvation may have cost us nothing, but true discipleship will cost us everything. It is for this reason, I suspect, that many over the centuries have left Christ and, by extension, His Church on earth. The cost was just too great. It is easy to leave a thing, far easier to leave a thing than a person, in fact. Consider the martyrs. They did not give their lives for a ritual but for relationship; they did not die for a "what" but for a whom.

Loving your "religion"

A lot of people have a difficult time with "religion." In one poll I read, more than 70 percent of people (even those who went to church) said they didn't think religion made the world a better place. In fact, as YouTube videos and blogs attest, many people are outright annoyed by *what they believe* religion to be (note the italics).

What's ironic is that the word "religion" comes from an ancient derivative of the word for **relationship**. Put simply, your relationship with God was made possible and carried out through "religious" practices and observances, such as participating in sacrifices and, later, in the sacraments. It was through religion that we came to have a relationship with God and His family, our fellowmen.

For many people, though, religion just seems to be a series of dos and don'ts, of archaic disciplines and constrictive rules you have to follow to keep from making God angry. Nothing could be further from the truth. Our Catholic faith, for instance, is designed to ensure you live in Christ (see Jn 10:10) and you do not die in sin (Rom 6:23). The Catholic faith invites you to a life of freedom, adventure, and true joy. The Catholic faith proclaims what Christ believes, that you are capable of becoming a saint through the grace available to you through His Church.

Catholicism is rooted in a relationship. Every sacrament is a means by which we grow in our relationship with Christ. Baptism establishes and initiates the relationship by our being adopted into God's family. The Eucharist we consume is Christ further showing us that He wants to be in union with us (communion). Confirmation is when the Spirit fully dwells in us so that we can remain constantly in relationship to God.

Our entire Catholic faith is an extension of the perpetual exchange of love between the Father, the Spirit, and Christ in the Trinity. We are created by this God, for this God. **We are created for relationship.**

Christ showed us that being in relationship is part of who we are. When He prayed the Lord's Prayer, the first line speaks of this relationship: "Our Father" (Mt 6:9). It wasn't as if He said only, "My Father." The fact that He included us when He addressed God says a lot. He told us it was the way that we ought to pray, reminding us that we are, indeed, a beloved son or daughter of a heavenly Father in heaven by virtue of our baptism and that the Cross makes Him available.

Christ did not need to be baptized in the Jordan, but offered us an example. That scene teaches us that when we ourselves are baptized, God says to each and every one of us, "You are my beloved son/daughter." With *you* God is well pleased.

Do you believe that God feels that way about you? Why?

Not only are you God's child, but you are also His beloved child. He isn't just a parent who cared *for you* (by providing food or shelter) but one who cares *about you*, wanting you to share every facet of your life with Him, every fear, joy, struggle, and success. He is the Father sitting in the family room waiting for you to get home and sit with Him. He is present, accessible, and interested. The love that God gives us is not distant or removed; His love is intimate, unconditional, and eternal.

This is our foundational identity (that we are a son or daughter of God), meaning that everything else flows from this truth. This reality affects the way that we interact with others in numerous ways. What we do with this reality, though, makes all the difference in life.

Do you remember that statement near the beginning of this chapter? Allow me to offer it, once again, in light of the rich young man and, in truth, in light of most of us (including myself):

> The urgency we assign to something is directly proportional to the value we place upon it.

How eagerly do you want to experience the deepest love God has to offer? How deeply do you desire life to the fullest? How far are you willing to go for God? Are you willing to open your hands and to let go of all this world offers in order to experience what the next promises?

In(to) your hands

Two young sons were arguing about how wise their father was. The older brother advised his younger brother to always listen to the father because his experience and wisdom were so great. The younger brother disagreed, however, stating: "Dad isn't that wise. I'm just as smart as he is, and I'll prove it." The younger brother then approached a tree and captured a small bird. He brought the bird home, went into the living room, and held the bird tightly in his cupped hands. The younger brother then posed the question to his father: "Dad, I have a small bird in my hands. Tell me, is he alive or dead?"

The younger brother had designed what he believed to be a foolproof plan. He'd decided that if the father replied "dead," he would just open his hands and let the bird fly away, proving his father wrong. If the father replied "alive," then the boy would crush the bird in his hands, revealing a dead bird upon opening them. The boys' father thought about the question for a moment, looked the younger son right in the eyes, and replied very sincerely, "Son, the answer is in your hands."

To bring life or to bring death on a daily basis, that ability, that answer, is in your hands. To walk in humility or be shackled by pride; to put God and others first or to expect the world to revolve around your every wish, desire, and reaction. Many — even Mass-going Catholics — claim to worship the Holy Trinity, but their schedules reveal that not to be the case. It's easy to say we follow the Father, Son, and Spirit when, in reality, we're busily infatuated with the minor trinity: me, myself, and I.

Jesus's challenge to the rich young man was an invitation rooted less in the surrender of the world than in surrendering to heaven. Christ was calling him into a daily and intimate relationship, without looking back.

The rich young man was all about action. If Christ had said, "Eternal life will cost you a thousand denarii," the young man would have promptly pulled out his moneybag. It would have required little, truthfully. Sure, perhaps the young man would have had to tighten his rope belt, but, in the end, it wouldn't have really required his heart.

In essence, Jesus was saying that eternal life would cost the rich young man a thousand denarii, paid out one coin at a time, one day at a time, for the rest of this life. The cost of eternal life is ongoing discipleship, constant conversion of heart, and reckless abandon to the will of the Father.

Still desire it? What earthly pleasures do you grasp? What counterfeit heavens and personal luxuries keep you from turning that corner in your faith life? You, like the young son mentioned in this story, have to look into your Father's eyes and make a life-or-death decision, right now.

Do you want to truly live, to live a life of abundance, allowing God to love you, Christ to forgive you, and the Holy Spirit to dwell in you? That "life" truly is in your hands. In the smallest of ways, many passing and seemingly unnoticeable, your life makes a difference every minute of every day, for better or for worse. The world is an ongoing play in which you play an integral part, even if you don't see it. Each moment the Lord is setting a choice before you, to follow Him and bring life, or to reject His truth and, resultantly, bring death. He's asking you, directly: "Do you want to abide in Me? Will you remain in Me? Do you desire to live in Me and allow Me to dwell within you?" These are questions everyone must ask, and it's a choice that everyone, especially everyone who calls himself or herself a Catholic or Christian, will make and MUST make.

> "I call heaven and earth to witness against you this day, that I have set before you life and death, blessing and curse; therefore choose life, that you and your descendants may live, loving the LORD your God, obeying his voice, and cleaving to him; for that means life to you and length of days." (Deuteronomy 30:19-20)

We all run into that proverbial road diverging into the wood with two paths to choose from. Many take the easy path, and why not? It's always easier not to sacrifice, not to forgive, not to love … but easy ain't the Gospel. The road to heaven is jagged and arduous and steep; the road to hell is paved with earthly gold and even has an HOV lane. Though Moses likely penned the above-inspired words from Deuteronomy well over three thousand years ago, they are as true in the twenty-first century as they were then. God's wisdom is good that way; it's both timeless and timely.

God, in His divine mercy, sets before us choices each day that offer us the opportunity to build up or to tear down, to bring life or to destroy it. God invites us to pray "thy kingdom come" as a reminder that "my kingdom (must) go." What mark on the world will your life leave this day? The answer, quite literally, is in YOUR hands … choose life.

A Step Beyond

Review your daily and weekly schedule. Look through your calendar, appointments, activities, and responsibilities.

Next, review your smartphone, emails, social-media posts and consumption, and your monthly bank statement.

Who and what have become "gods" in your life? Where does your time and treasure go? What monopolizes your attention? Where has earth taken precedence over heaven and diverted your eyes from upward to downward to inward?

It's always easier not to sacrifice, not to forgive, not to love ... but easy ain't the Gospel.

Identify any false gods that have taken over your life. Name them, claim them, and then have the courage to prayerfully let them go. We cannot taste heaven if we are constantly clutching the hems and robes of false gods.

Clasped and closed hands signal death. Open hands usher in life.

Choose wisely.

Chapter 6

Encountering Jesus Affirms Your Great Worth

Christ and Zacchaeus

A couple of years ago, I was downtown in a big city (that will remain unnamed) rushing to get to a weekday morning Mass between meetings. On the way up the steps of the cathedral I passed a homeless man asking for money. Though rushed, I offered to buy him breakfast; he refused to come with me, saying he wasn't hungry. I invited him to come with me to Mass. He declined. I asked if he wanted to talk or pray right there. He refused … telling me that God had abandoned him and that "if God was really loving He would never have let so many bad things happen."

It was a gut-wrenching conversation that I told him I wanted to continue over coffee or a meal after Mass. I asked him to wait for me, as I'd be free to talk more in about thirty minutes. He declined that invitation, too.

Upon entering the church, still thinking about the soul I'd just encountered, I found myself seated among a smattering of different people: a nurse between shifts, some elderly couples, a young mom wrestling with her little kids, a couple of nuns, some tourists, and a handful of professionals beginning their workday with God's greatest act of love (which we call the Mass).

Moments after I sat, in walked another (slightly tardy) Catholic, out of breath and rushing in so as not to miss the readings. I recognized him (as we had met on a few occasions) and motioned for him to sit next to me. He was a fairly well-known and highly respected businessman, as well as a godly husband and father. Incidentally, he's also a millionaire (which is important to the story, so stick with me).

Redefining poverty

Now, the man outside the church and the man sitting beside me could not have been more different economically … one rich and one poor, right? The most intriguing difference between the two souls, however, was (the posture of) their souls.

Now, I am in no way judging either man. God alone is judge (see 2 Cor 5:10; Mt 7:1). Based upon the conversations I had with each, though, I'd like to draw a comparison. In terms of spirituality, the millionaire praying beside me may have been far more "impoverished" than the homeless man on the steps, because true poverty extends far beyond the wallet.

When Our Lord gave us the Sermon on the Mount, He began with the beatitudes (see Mt 5:1-11), and in those beatitudes He began with this proclamation:

> "Blessed are the poor in spirit, for theirs is the kingdom of heaven." (v. 3)

This is one of those Scripture passages that many people "know" (meaning, they've heard it before) but countless people fail to understand. My own parochial schoolteacher taught us that it simply meant God loves poor people "more."

Ummm ... to put it as charitably and bluntly as possible ... no, that's not what it means.

God does not love anybody "more" than another. God loves the prostitute as much as the pope, the pagan as much as the priest, the atheist as much as the greatest saint. God is perfect love (see 1 Jn 4:8). His love is fatherly, not fickle. Sin destroys the relationship, though, as it deadens our capacity to both love and receive God's love. Our personal sin does not, however, in any way, reduce His love for us.

It's only when we realize how badly we need God and how we are nothing without Him that we become worthy of the kingdom He promises us.

That being said, physical poverty (material and financial) is often associated with holiness. Jesus praised the economically poor on more than one occasion (see Lk 4:18; 7:22; Mt 11:5), and He shared in physical hardship, often living in a destitute way (Mt 21:18; Jn 4:6-7; Lk 9:58). Truthfully, the Incarnation itself is a living example of poverty as God emptied himself and took on flesh (2 Cor 8:9; Phil 2:7-8).

Now, the phrase "poor in spirit" speaks to an even deeper reality, beyond physical poverty, to true spiritual poverty. To be poor in spirit means to acknowledge our deepest human need for God and to grow in that longing and that dependence on a daily basis. It's only when we realize how badly we need God and how we are nothing without Him that we become worthy of the kingdom He promises us (see Mt 5:3). It's when we realize we are the beggars that our gratitude to the Giver (of life) becomes that much greater.

The Old Testament speaks in several places of this longing for God and His faithfulness in our spiritual poverty. Take a few minutes and pray through Psalms 34:6, Isaiah 61:1, and Zephaniah 2:3, to name a few. The root of this teaching on spiritual poverty isn't just reserved to the Old Testament, either.

Remember why the rich young man went away downcast (see Mk 10:17-31)? Do you recall why the widow was so praised by Jesus (Lk 21:1-4)? Do you remember what the apostles were supposed to take with them and rely on during their missionary work (Mk 6:7-12)? Jesus even teaches that loving the poor is a condition we must fulfill if we are to enter His kingdom (Mt 25:31-46).

So what about the rich? We've already discussed the rich young man — rich by inheritance, hard work, or blind luck. What, though, is God's posture toward those who have gotten rich at the expense of the poor? It might surprise you.

Scaling sycamore

> He entered Jericho and was passing through. And there was a man named Zacchaeus; he was a chief tax collector, and rich. And he sought to see who Jesus was, but could not, on account of the crowd, because he was small of stature. So he ran on ahead and climbed up into a sycamore tree to see him, for he was to pass that way. And when Jesus came to the place, he looked up and said to him, "Zacchaeus, make haste and come down; for I must stay at your house today." So he made haste and came down, and received him joyfully. And when they saw it they all murmured, "He has gone in to be the guest of a man who is a sinner." And Zacchaeus stood and said to the

> Lord, "Behold, Lord, the half of my goods I give to the poor; and if I have defrauded any one of anything, I restore it fourfold." And Jesus said to him, "Today salvation has come to this house, since he also is a son of Abraham. For the Son of man came to seek and to save the lost." (Luke 19:1-10)

Perhaps never in the history of humanity were splinters from climbing a tree such a blessing. Never before had pain been so fleeting or so worth it. Jesus was passing through Jericho, and this tax collector, Zacchaeus, wanted to be front and center on the parade route. To really appreciate this brief but powerful episode, however, it's important not to miss a single Holy Spirit-inspired detail.

We're told, "he was a chief tax collector, and rich." Tax collectors in the time of Jesus weren't just the biblical equivalent of the IRS … they were far, far worse. In fact, tax collectors were among the most despised within a community. In an effort to maximize Roman profit while minimizing their personnel's time, the Roman government would recruit local Jews and offer them a percentage of the taxes collected from their kin and countrymen. If a tax collector was particularly ruthless or dishonest, his percentage would exponentially grow; basically, the more blood they could squeeze from their neighbors, the more they could keep. Worse yet was that the money they took was then used by the Romans to further oppress the Jewish people — God's people! Not only was Zacchaeus a tax collector, he was their chief. The buck stopped with him (meaning the bucks also flowed to him).

Next we hear:

> And he sought to see who Jesus was, but could not, on account of the crowd, because he was small of

> stature. So he ran on ahead and climbed up into a sycamore tree to see him, for he was to pass that way. (Luke 19:3-4)

While Zacchaeus may have been long on zeal and initiative, he was short in stature, so while the streets filled with onlookers, he was forced to act out of character. The one used to fixing the scales in the customs booth was now fixing to scale a sycamore tree, just for the chance at a glance of the wonderworker whose reputation was obviously now preceding Him.

What made him climb the tree that day? Sure, Zacchaues was short, but that's still a lot to go through just to see someone. Yes, Jesus was developing a quasi — "rock star" — celebrity status. But tree climbing? It was so impulsive, so uncivilized, and, quite frankly, so seemingly out of character. Or was it? What kind of heart beat beneath Zacchaeus's unapologetic and self-centered exterior?

Have you ever had "everything" and realized that, in reality, you had nothing? Have you ever taken a chance on God, putting yourself "out there"?

Just a few verses later we learn that Zacchaeus is an admitted cheat, fraudulently taking more taxes from the people than was prescribed. Why would someone so willfully in the wrong so desperately want to experience "the right"? Others in the town had heard of Jesus. Many turned out. Many did not. For countless others, Jesus wasn't worth the time. There was work to be done, and there were lives to be led. So why was Zacchaeus different? Why did grace move in his heart on this particular day, getting him to drop what he was doing and put himself in a position for the Lord to speak to him?

Have you ever done that? Have you ever had "everything" and realized that, in reality, you had nothing? Have you ever taken a chance on God, putting yourself "out there"? Reading books like this one might be the first (or fiftieth) step. Maybe you tuned in to a Catholic radio channel and left it there without knowing why. Perhaps you stumbled into a local church just to see if someone would notice or anything might "stick." Who knows, maybe you went online to refute a claim or a thought that you found disagreeable only to have it speak to your heart in ways you weren't prepared to receive. No matter the instance, the impetus was the same, and it's usually the Holy Spirit. Who knows why we do half the things we do? God knows, and He is working for our salvation even when we are not.

The daring, dining Deity

So up the tree our swindler went, and little did he know what a branch he was really treading on that day, for Zacchaeus was about to throw possibly the greatest impromptu dinner party in salvation history.

Let's review: Zacchaeus climbed a tree for Jesus. That's all it took, really. He put forth the effort to see God. God noticed … and responded in kind. How ironic it is that all the while Zacchaeus was seeking Jesus — like the Magi, the fisherman, and the well-wisher before him — God was actually seeking him. Where Jesus went, the Kingdom came with Him, and this night, the Kingdom was setting up shop at la casa de Zacchaeus.

> And when Jesus came to the place, he looked up and said to him, "Zacchaeus, make haste and come down; for I must stay at your house today." So he made haste and came down, and received him joyfully. And when

they saw it they all murmured, "He has gone in to be the guest of a man who is a sinner." (vv. 5-7)

What's even more interesting and far more daring on Jesus's part is His break from cultural convention, yet again. If a Jew knowingly entered the house of a sinner — which we see Our Lord not only suggesting but *commanding* — that Jew was, then, ritually impure and unclean. While we have the benefit of divine revelation offering us twenty-twenty perspective, the onlookers in Jericho did not. This would not have been merely intriguing or odd but absolutely shocking behavior! Luckily for Christ, the purest purity cannot be made impure by anything or anyone. Put simply, purity had nothing to fear and the sinner had everything to gain; Zacchaeus may have been up a tree, literally, but he no longer had to be up a creek, spiritually.

There is no greater affirmation the Lord could give him or us, this side of heaven, than to say He wants to stay with us.

Our Lord's seemingly rude and quite bold self-invitation was anything but. Jesus offered Zacchaeus, the taxman, not an exemption but complete redemption. In imposing a financial yoke upon others, Zacchaeus's greed had placed a guilt-ridden yoke of self-centeredness upon himself. Now, the carpenter who most likely fashioned yokes as part of his carpentry business in Nazareth was offering to exchange the yoke of slavery to sin for a yoke of mercy, forgiveness, and grace.

Note, too, that (unlike the rich young man) Zacchaeus responded with haste and urgency. The wealth and — more to the point, the dishonesty — was anchoring Zacchaeus; the guilt and burden left him unable to move or truly live. Picture the cheater almost leaping down from the tree thinking, "***He*** wants to be with ***me***?!?"

The God of the universe wanted to break bread with this sinful soul.

Is there a higher affirmation on the planet? In the cosmos? The Creator of creation wants to dine with you, to break bread with you, to talk to you and listen to you and forgive you and share company with you.

Has anything really changed?

"This man receives sinners and eats with them" (Lk 15:2).

Yes, He does … at every single Mass.

And when we receive Jesus, we — like Zacchaeus — ought to receive Him joyfully.

There is no greater affirmation the Lord could give him or us, this side of heaven, than to say He wants to stay with us.

Look, too, at the response of the sinful soul, after beholding and experiencing the Lord at the table:

> And Zacchaeus stood and said to the Lord, "Behold, Lord, the half of my goods I give to the poor; and if I have defrauded any one of anything, I restore it fourfold." And Jesus said to him, "Today salvation has come to this house, since he also is a son of Abraham. For the Son of man came to seek and to save the lost." (vv. 8-10)

Let's not miss the life-altering, soul-stirring magnitude of what transpired over a random dinner one night so many centuries ago:

Sin was transformed by grace.

A heart returned to God.

Charity was offered and charity rightly followed.

The love of money — which is the "root of all evil" as St. Paul reminds us — was supplanted by a love of mercy. Consider what Zacchaeus was giving up: his financial security, his professional future, and quite possibly his personal safety at the mercy of those he'd cheated. Let it go Zacchaeus did, however, and he did it with style. He would pay it all back *and then some*. He would go above and beyond. He would let it all go — as long as it meant that the mercy would remain. Zacchaeus learned that night what the rich young man and countless since need to learn. If you want to hold on to Christ, you must be willing to let go of all else. One cannot grasp heaven when clutching earth. Fear cannot exist where true love dwells.

Perhaps that's why Zacchaeus was so trusting of God … because he wasn't trying to "earn" God's favor. Zacchaeus was obviously aware of his own sin and his own need for mercy. He just responded to the grace of God. Zacchaeus responded to the invitation.

Do you?

Have you responded to the invitation of God, to begin your life again? Have you answered God's call to reconcile your past, that you might experience an all-new future in Him? While Jesus might not be walking down your street calling your name, make no mistake that He is always calling, always pursuing. The Good Shepherd doesn't stand still; He pursues. Ironically, it takes us being still to actually realize or appreciate just how fervently God desires us (see Ps 46:10-11).

One might even suspect that Zacchaeus would have tried to control the situation as so many of us do, that he may have tried to somehow "earn" God's mercy with a fat tithe or crooked contribution. To be clear, Christ offered mercy and forgiveness well before Zacchaeus announced his intended restitution. We cannot buy what God offers freely. We cannot earn our inheritance. All we can do is humbly accept and graciously offer back to God His own unrequited and most pure love. Zacchaeus's reparation was a response to God's mercy.

Even though the invite came by way of Jesus's prompting, it was an invite nonetheless. The carpenter didn't kick the door in or take the door off its hinges. The sinner invited the Savior in; heaven stood knocking on the door of Zacchaeus's heart, and the merciless responded to mercy. Opening that door required a willingness to change, though, and it still does. You can't invite Jesus to visit but not to dwell. It's when we invite Jesus merely to stop by to heal, but not to stay and save, that we miss the chance at true life. To experience Jesus is to breathe pure oxygen in a world of smog, but *to know and walk with Jesus*, daily, **that** is to truly live.

A reward worth the risk

Many mistake the Bible's purpose. Bumper-sticker theology and trite clichés tell us that the Bible teaches us how to live. Nothing could be further from the truth. Self-help books make suggestions on how to live, but sacred Scripture doesn't counsel us to become more independent, but, rather, more *dependent* (on God). Simply put, the Bible doesn't teach us how to live as much as it models for us how to die — to our sin, to our selfishness, and to this world. It's only when we come to grips with death to the world that we realize how much richer we are when we live for heaven.

The chief tax collector learned his lesson, and his story invites us to do the same. Zacchaeus climbed a tree to catch a glimpse of mercy. Mercy got nailed to a tree to offer Zacchaeus a glimpse of heaven — and the love-filled sacrifice it requires to get there. That day, salvation came knocking. How many days has salvation come knocking, come seeking *you*? Through the radio, the television, the Internet, a personal invitation to go (even) deeper in the Faith and with God?

How many days has salvation come knocking, come seeking you? *Through the radio, the television, the Internet, a personal invitation to go (even) deeper in the Faith and with God?*

He stands at the door of your heart, knocking (see Rv 3:20). Picking up this book, you scaled a sycamore. The question is whether or not you want the adventure to continue. Do you have the courage now to come down and to live even more abandoned to Christ?

It was actually a win-win situation for Zacchaeus that night. He had much to lose but so, so much more to gain. He didn't get paralyzed with fear as we do, though. He was so aware of his own deeper longing for love and validation and to feel worthy in the eyes of heaven that Christ raised the bar on Zacchaeus, and the tax collector from Jericho rose to the occasion. Examples like his should cause us to consider some hard questions in our own walks with the Lord:

- Would *you* risk embarrassment, your reputation, or even your job for the sake of Jesus?
- Are you willing to do anything different in order to see Jesus more clearly?
- Is the crowd around you the reason you can't see Jesus clearly?
- Are you afraid to break from your routine or your comfort zone?

- When Christ looks at you and calls your name, do you respond or look away?
- When God knocks, do you invite him in?
- When the Spirit convicts your heart, do you admit your wrongdoing or redirect blame?
- Are you seeking only personal forgiveness, or do you desire to make restitution to those you have hurt along the way?

The answers to these questions reveal whether our collective desire is riches on earth or riches in heaven. Are we poor financially or spiritually? Which reveals a greater *dependency*?

Poor us

Remember my earlier tale of two poor men: the beggar and the millionaire?

That day at the cathedral I encountered great poverty, to be sure, both outside the church and within its walls. Poverty exists everywhere in our world, on park benches and in cardboard boxes as well as within penthouse apartments and suburban homes. Pope Francis's call to the modern world has been consistently laced and underpinned with the call to love the poor, yes, but *also* to acknowledge our own spiritual poverty in the wake of secularism, humanism, and pluralism. His example has been challenging, and his call to the Church harrowing, to say the least.

The key isn't whether you have money or not, but whether you have God or not. As the great St. Francis de Sales put it in his *Introduction to the Devout Life* (which is a must-read, by the way):

> Woe then to those who are rich in spirit, for their portion will be hell. He is rich in spirit whose heart is in his riches, and whose riches fill his heart ... if you possess them, preserve your heart from loving them. Do not, then, complain of your poverty (if you are poor), for we complain only of that which displeases us; and if poverty displeases you, you are no longer poor in spirit, for your heart would rather be otherwise.

Like the earthly millionaire praying beside me that day, so blessed are those who realize their constant need for God above and beyond everything else. To be fair, too, my friend died giving it all away. At the foot of the Lord's altar, each day, this man learned not solely to give from his excess (financially) but to give from his constant poverty of soul, to give his everything *spiritually*.

A Step Beyond

Looking at your calendar, bank account, and schedule, is there more you could give? Are you a good steward of all God has entrusted to you? We often are asked to "give 10 percent" (which is where we get the term "tithe," meaning "one-tenth"). Do we look at it as "I'm giving 10 percent" or, rather, "God lets me keep 90 percent!" Look at it as…? (Totally waiting for that finish.)

Where might you bless the Church on earth by giving more freely of your time, your talent, and, most notably, your treasure? Note that during the recent economic and real estate market crises the souls least stressed were those with the least amount to lose.

How truly blessed are those not chained to the material and passing pleasures and luxuries of this finite world? Blessed are those free from anything and everything that would interfere with an ever-growing awe of God's mercy and love. Blessed are those who recognize that no matter how their life is going in the eyes of the world, they are successful in heaven when they are faithful on earth. Blessed are those who need nothing more than God's love and want nothing more than to share that love with all they encounter.

A soul with nothing to lose on earth is a wonderfully dangerous soul, a soul that will lead many to heaven. Truly blessed are the poor in spirit.

Chapter 7

Encountering Jesus Invites You to Serve

Christ and the Woman Who Washed His Feet

As night fell on this particular Saturday, I felt pretty good about myself. I had accomplished all twelve of the tasks on my wife's "honey do" list. I'd hung drapes, moved shelves, replaced the disposal, and fixed the dryer. You name it, I'd done it ... and all without waking the baby from a nap or one trip to the emergency room. I was a regular suburban ninja with laser focus and silent efficiency, wielding not a sword but a tool belt. As I poured a well-deserved glass of wine and my exhausted body retreated to the couch beside my bride, I had no idea the real service had yet to begin.

Not two sips into the wine my wife began to share the struggles she had faced that day. She talked about personal feelings, physical ailments, discipline issues with the kids, and stresses around the house. All valid, all important, and all very fixable for a handy guy like me. I quickly offered idea after idea, insight after insight on how to solve each of her problems in an orderly and ninjaesque fashion. My thoughts were met not with accolades but with saddened silence. She needed to share a problem, but I was far too concerned with sharing my solutions.

To be honest, it's far easier for me to show my love for my wife through accomplishing a list of tasks than for me to just sit on the couch and be present to her for long conversations. The "honey do" list is far preferable to the "honey, be" invitation. Tell me what frame to hang, but don't just ask me to hang out. As the groom, it's a constant, daily struggle for me to just slow down and share space with my bride. It's for this reason that wives, through the ages, after sharing their hearts with semi-distracted husbands, have uttered the words, "I don't want you to fix it; I just want you to *listen*." Ah, the art of presence, so often lost on the go-getters. Obviously, it's not just a male issue, either.

Thou shalt not serve?

Do you remember the story of Sts. Martha and Mary? Of course you do ... every good Catholic has heard at least one homily in their lifetime praising Mary who sat at the Lord's feet while her sister Martha (patron saint of waiters and waitresses ... true story) scurries around waiting on Jesus. As we see in Martha, doing is always easier (and often preferable) to *being*.

Let's have another look:

> Now as they went on their way, he entered a village; and a woman named Martha received him into her house. And she had a sister called Mary, who sat at the Lord's feet and listened to his teaching. But Martha was distracted with much serving; and she went to him and said, "Lord, do you not care that my sister has left me to serve alone? Tell her then to help me." But the Lord answered her, "Martha, Martha, you are

> anxious and troubled about many things; one thing is needful. Mary has chosen the good portion, which shall not be taken away from her." (Luke 10:38-42)

Martha usually gets a pretty bad rap. Consider what the story tells us: She was serving the Lord. Apparently, Martha's "love language" was "acts of service." Moreover, hospitality is foundational in Mediterranean culture. To serve another was a way of honoring them, your people, your culture, and your God. Not only was this how she showed her love for her God, but this was expected culturally. If anything, one would think that Mary is the one who'd have been getting the roll of Christ's divine eyes! Yet, it's with this backdrop that Jesus corrects Martha?

We really are a culture of human doings and not human beings.

Shakespeare offered, "To be or not to be," as the more important question. In this scene, however, the Lord seems to offer a different question altogether: Is it better to be or to do?

Martha serves and Mary sits. And Martha gets scolded? This is where control freaks (like myself) come unraveled. As mentioned before, it's far easier to show love through tasks than through complete and utter emotional presence. Tasks require energy, but truly serving the other necessitates far more and is a gift from the heart. We really are a culture of human doings and not human beings.

Truthfully, you'll still find this mindset in many parish ministries and homes, with souls who are far more comfortable doing than praying, far more at ease serving than just being. It's the great challenge of the Christian life, especially for leaders and Type A personalities. It's far easier to love others in the name of Christ than it is to just sit and *be loved by Christ* in our daily prayer time. We replace our prayer with projects, our contemplation with completed tasks, and wonder, "Where is God? I can't hear Him (whom I am serving)."

As Venerable Fulton Sheen reminded us, "Ever since the days of Adam, man has been hiding from God and saying, 'God is hard to find.'" Sometimes we get too busy to notice the God of the universe right before us. Sometimes we are so easily distracted we may not even recognize our God upon the altar or being offered to us at the end of the Communion line.

The exact opposite is true of Christ, the bridegroom. He is constantly present, ever available to His bride, the Church. He is waiting and desiring the most intimate relationship possible with each and every one of us. His presence in the Eucharist is an invitation to prayer and, more to the point, to intimacy.

Fascinatingly, during his visit to Australia for World Youth Day in 2008, Pope Benedict XVI expounded upon this concept that we must first "be" (receive Christ) before we can "do" (offer Christ):

> These gifts of the Spirit … are neither prizes nor rewards. They are freely given (cf. 1 Cor 12:11). And they require only one response on the part of the receiver: I accept! **Here we sense something of the deep mystery of being Christian. What constitutes our faith is not primarily what we do but what we receive.** After all, many generous people who are not Christian may well achieve far more than we do. Friends, do you accept being drawn into God's Trinitarian life … his communion of love? (emphasis added)

Do you see what he said there? This is more than just saying, "You can't give what you don't have." In essence, this is Christ saying, "It's better to receive than to give," or more to the point, to be a true Christian it's a necessity to receive Christ and the gifts of the Spirit if you desire to give to others ... otherwise our giving will be dis-ordered.

Anyone can serve the poor. Atheists could conceivably be far more active and benevolent than many Christians in this way. What makes us Christian, though, is supposed to be the "why" we do it, the "Whom" we do it for, and the "Who" that empowers us to serve! If we show up to serve at the parish or in our community but haven't prayed about why, it's not necessarily God whom we're doing it for — it's not glorifying the Holy Trinity as much as it is an exercise of praise for the minor trinity.

It's far easier to love others in the name of Christ than it is to just sit and be loved by Christ in our daily prayer time.

When we pray, however, and when we consistently seek Jesus in the sacraments, most specifically in the Eucharist through Mass and adoration, all of our acts of service in our homes, schools, offices, and parishes ***flow from*** our interior prayer life and the altar, and are thus rightly ordered. In short, our doing (acts of service) will be truly pure because it will be a response to our being (times of prayer).

It is with this understanding that we turn attention to our next Scripture story, set at yet another dinner party, when an unexpected guest shows "the holy ones" what true holiness looks like.

A jar-ing scene

> Now when Jesus was at Bethany in the house of Simon the leper, a woman came up to him with an alabaster jar of very expensive ointment, and she poured it on his head, as he sat at table. But when the disciples saw it, they were indignant, saying, "Why this waste? For this ointment might have been sold for a large sum, and given to the poor." But Jesus, aware of this, said to them, "Why do you trouble the woman? For she has done a beautiful thing to me. For you always have the poor with you, but you will not always have me. In pouring this ointment on my body she has done it to prepare me for burial. Truly, I say to you, wherever this gospel is preached in the whole world, what she has done will be told in memory of her." (Matthew 26:6-13)

It's a beautiful story, is it not? Some unnamed woman is so overwhelmed by God's beauty and goodness that she crashes the dinner party to anoint and bathe the God before them. This is the kind of scene that reality television seeks and often contrives — raw human emotion free of social decorum. It is both a gorgeous act of devotion and an intimate act of adoration. No shame or guilt would stop this heart so overflowing with love for God. If only we could all bring such passion and reckless abandon to the foot of the altar each and every Sunday when we approach the Lord at table!

Even more fascinating to me, though, is what we learn about the identity of this woman spoken about by St. Matthew through the Holy Spirit and penned by St. John. In the parallel story given to us by Jesus's closest disciple,

John the beloved, we are given a glorious glimpse into the identity of this anonymous anointer:

> Six days before the Passover, Jesus came to Bethany, where Lazarus was, whom Jesus had raised from the dead. There they made him a supper; Martha served, and Lazarus was one of those at table with him. Mary took a pound of costly ointment of pure nard and anointed the feet of Jesus and wiped his feet with her hair; and the house was filled with the fragrance of the ointment. But Judas Iscariot, one of his disciples (he who was to betray him), said, "Why was this ointment not sold for three hundred denarii and given to the poor?" This he said, not that he cared for the poor but because he was a thief, and as he had the money box he used to take what was put into it. Jesus said, "Let her alone, let her keep it for the day of my burial. The poor you always have with you, but you do not always have me." (John 12:1-8)

While the Gospel accounts vary on certain details and some scholars may disagree, it is more than plausible — it is literally inspired and recorded by St. John — that the woman who anointed Christ prior to his own death and "washed" the Lord's feet at table days before He would wash His apostles' feet, was none other than Mary of Bethany, sister of Martha and Lazarus. This is yet another reason that reading all of the Gospels and paying attention to details is the only way to get a truly accurate perspective on this Jesus we hear so much about. If we do not read Scripture, the danger is that the Jesus we come face to face with will be your pastor's Jesus, your professor's Jesus, or your catechist's Jesus, but not necessarily the *true Jesus* as He is revealing himself to you through the Holy Spirit.

Why is this detail so important to comprehending the story? Why is the identity of the divine foot washer and sacred skull anointer so important to know? Because as Pope Emeritus Benedict XVI reminded us, it is only *after we receive* that we can rightly give. It is only after we have received the mercy of God, the grace (life) of God, and the presence of God that we can truly be empowered to serve in His name. In short, our doing must flow forth from our being. To act or serve without first beholding the sacred mystery that is God is a disordered act. This is the very reason that Blessed Mother Teresa of Calcutta insisted that her Missionaries of Charity should spend a full hour in adoration of the Blessed Sacrament (the Eucharist) *every single morning* ***prior*** to their efforts to serve the world's poor. Did the poor not have needs during that sixty minutes? Of course they did. Would it not have been a beautiful, merciful act to feed them for an additional sixty minutes? Sure. What Mother Teresa understood, however, was that if the service did not constantly flow from the altar of mercy, eventually that river of mercy would cease to flow.

You have nothing to give but Christ in you. Everything else you offer will, in time, break, fade, distract, or die. The only thing about you that is all yours, the only thing about you that is not a blessing from God, is your sin. Everything else you have to offer is a gift from God. We have nothing eternal to offer except the presence of Christ within us. We can offer the Holy Spirit, whom Pope Benedict called "the soul of our soul." Everything else is fleeting. Christ, alone, is eternal.

Bare(ly) minimum

A large red C- was scribbled atop the term paper that sat on the passenger seat next to me. As I pulled into the driveway of my house, terror gripped my teenage body. My parents, who expected an A every time, sat inside eating dinner. I knew full well that I was capable of an A, but, in all honesty, I hadn't really applied myself. The problem was, my parents also knew I was capable of the A. Being good parents, they never wanted me to settle for less than I could be. So the entire drive home was an interior monologue in which I ran down a litany of excuses I would offer them to cover up the reality of academic laziness.

"The average grade in the class was a D," I offered my parents as I handed them my paper. "There weren't any As or Bs given in the whole class. So, with the curve, it's like I got an A," I said, justifying my grade not only to them, but also to myself.

They nodded their heads in suspicious agreement. Not much more was said, but their looks spoke volumes. They were not disappointed in the C-, but rather in their son, who they knew had not completely applied himself.

> *We have nothing eternal to offer except the presence of Christ within us. We can offer the Holy Spirit, whom Pope Benedict called "the soul of our soul."*

"As long as you did your best," they replied in a tone that tore my flesh to the very bone. It was as though I could feel my heart being ripped from my chest in their gentle tone and seemingly reassuring nods. I may have dodged the bullet on my grade, but it cost me something I desired and cherished even more — the respect and approval of my parents.

No, I hadn't done my best on that paper, and thank God for the grading curve in that class. (What I actually mean is, "Thank God for a classroom filled with other unmotivated teenagers who surrounded me at the time." But let's not digress.) The lack of interest in my classmates made my own laziness less apparent. The C- was good enough — it was still better than most of the class. At least, it was until this particular night. All of the sudden, the normal excuse had worn thin. I realized that I had used it too many times. My parents were not buying it anymore. I could do better. I knew it. They knew it. All I had to do was admit it. It wasn't enough to recognize that I wasn't living up to my potential. I actually had to discipline myself and do the work. I needed to start giving my best effort, every time.

The more I got to thinking — and praying — that night, it occurred to me that I had often approached God in the same way. I hadn't given my best. I hadn't given even close to my best effort, really. I allowed the lack of holiness in those around me to dictate my own pursuit of holiness. I didn't seek out accountability; I sought comfort. I didn't apply myself completely to my schoolwork or my faith; I took what came easy. I did what I had to do, what I wanted to do, but rarely what I actually needed to do. I was content living on and with "the curve," where little was asked of me and even less was expected. I sought comfort at every turn, ease at every intersection of life, and now, finally, my sloth had caught up with me.

I don't think I was alone in this way, either. We don't really pursue the Lord with everything. It's okay to be "into" your faith, that is, until it causes others to be uncomfortable. It's when your faith becomes dangerous — around the office, on social media, or at awkward Thanksgiving dinners

— that you go from being labeled "religious" to outright "dangerous" and fanatical. So our response is to embrace the curve and hide amongst the rest of the unmotivated classmates around us. We use their lack of spiritual acumen as yet another excuse to make ourselves look better. As a society, we not only justify our mediocrity, we attempt to sanctify it.

When lions become lambs

Not only have many become meek about their faith in the public square, they are becoming weak. We stand up until we stand out. We're more comfortable serving the food than bathing the feet. It appears more noble to do so. Serving others all night? Yes, I'm comfortable with that. Publicly adoring the one true God of the universe with every fiber of our being? Let's not get fanatical here, right? Put the cork back in the alabaster jar … our reckless devotion ought not make anyone uncomfortable.

Is that really the goal of faith? Is this the focus of our life? Comfort?

Consider what Jesus said after He washed the feet of His disciples:

> "For I have given you an example, that you also should do as I have done to you." (John 13:15)

Verses like this one cut right through the excuses we offer the world for the sin and selfishness we allow in our lives. Jesus could not put it more simply. Here, He gives us a window into the Father's heart. He's saying: "I give my everything — all of myself — every single time. I hold nothing back, nor should you." A day later, upon the cross, Christ put the exclamation point on this very fact.

God the Father knows what we're capable of — He created us. He wants us to realize and become all that we can be through the power of the Holy Spirit, not just to settle for all that we currently are. God does grade on a curve, but it's shaped like a cross.

Picture it this way: Your report card hangs on the Father's refrigerator. Only the two of you know if you've done your best. The good news is that a minus becomes a plus the minute you pray. The better news is that God gives you the grace necessary to become a saint if you're willing to live for the A every day.

To serve the Lord is a high privilege, but to adore the Lord is the highest praise. The saints, through their devotion and virtue, set the bar high for the rest of us.

As the great French novelist and poet Leon Bloy once penned, "The only real sadness, the only real failure, the only great tragedy in life, is not to become a saint." He knew well how deadly judging and living our lives on "the curve" could be. Sts. Martha and Mary offer us invaluable insight into discipleship. To serve the Lord is a high privilege, but to adore the Lord is the highest praise. The saints, through their devotion and virtue, set the bar high for the rest of us. The saints destroy the curve, revealing to us not that they are "holier than thou" but that the power of grace can turn even the most egregious of sinners into the greatest of saints.

St. Mary of Bethany refused to do so. She came face to face with God, acknowledged her sin, experienced his mercy, and allowed that to fuel her every action and desire, regardless of public perception, scorn, or judgment.

Mary sets the bar high, challenging each of us to ascend to it.

A Step Beyond

Identify those areas in your life in which you may be slothful (spiritually lazy). What are some ways you can let the Holy Spirit unleash new layers of greatness from within you? Write them out. Share them with people you know and trust who will hold you accountable. Raise your spiritual bar and keep it high.

And know this: in destroying "the curve" for the other souls in your life, you are actually helping them grow closer to Christ. God can do more with your example than you can. Embrace humility. Seek holiness. Smash the alabaster jar and hold nothing back. God deserves your best effort — all that you are — every single day. If you woke up with air in your lungs, it is a sure sign He's not done with you yet. Give your best to God, daily, because He deserves it.

Chapter 8

Encountering Jesus Offers You Hope

Christ and Jairus

"He will need to be restrained for this," the nurse explained to my wife and me. Just one week after the birth of our son, we were back in the hospital with him as he fought a serious infection. His fever was spiking, his kidneys were taxed, and his tiny body was writhing in pain during the spinal tap. His beautiful hands and feet became bruised from the IV/PICC lines. He wanted to be held but had to undergo test after test. Standing there draped in lead jackets for *our* protection, I was now holding down my wailing baby boy as he was strapped to a board and slowly moved into the imaging machine. Standing there, hopeful yet helpless, our love for this tiny soul reached new levels. It's astounding how painful it can be to watch another — especially a little one — suffer.

As a father, I wanted to pull the still-beating heart from my chest and offer it in place of his — I would have given anything, *anything* to trade places with him. The world has it wrong when it says, "If God were *truly good* there wouldn't be any more suffering." That day gave me new appreciation for the Cross and new insight into our heavenly Father. We focus on Christ's sacrifice on Good Friday — and rightly so — but how often do we focus on the sacrifice of the Father, giving His only Son, perfect and blameless, as a ransom for the rest of His children who are far from sinless? How often do we pause to contemplate the magnitude of what heaven offered earth that Friday? I caught a glimpse of something glorious in the midst of my own tears and suffering: I was given the smallest glimpse of God the Father's love for us. Suffering reveals not the absence of love but the truest depths of it.

Perhaps you, like me, have held an anxious mother in that gut-wrenching moment when the ultrasound shows that the heartbeat has stopped. Maybe you, too, have sat bedside with that loved one in hospice care, clinging to sacred moments where life is thrust into perspective as one soul passes from here to life eternal. Maybe you have also held a child who's experienced bullying or comforted a friend suffering through a divorce. Maybe you have supported and aided a loved one as their body aged faster than their mind or cheered on a special-needs body with a heroic heart. It's in these moments that our humanity really comes into focus, isn't it? It's in these moments when life slows to a pause that we taste our own mortality. We come face to face with our deep-seated vices and seemingly distant virtues and are called on the carpet before God and man about who we *really are*, the point of life, and who He designed us to be.

Suffering was (and is) certainly personal to Jesus.

When the person suffering is beside you, within breathing distance, able to peer into your eyes as you gaze into theirs, that's when suffering goes from universal to quite personal. Suffering was (and is) certainly personal to Jesus.

We read several episodes of distraught parents in the Gospels. In one, Jesus was passing through Nain and came across a poor widow who had recently lost her only son. In another episode, we read of Jesus coming down off the mountain following the Transfiguration. While the apostles are still trying to wrap their minds around Christ's radiant glory, Jesus was approached by a father with a problem — a child with a demon. Parents always want more for their kids than themselves. Good parents want their kids not only to succeed professionally but to be happy, healthy, and holy. Parents want, more than anything else, for their children to truly *live*.

Family matters

One of the most poignant and touching scenes for me has always been the story of the synagogue official Jairus, who draws near to Jesus seeking healing for his ailing daughter as she is near death.

> And when Jesus had crossed again in the boat to the other side, a great crowd gathered about him; and he was beside the sea. Then came one of the rulers of the synagogue, Jairus by name; and seeing him, he fell at his feet, and besought him, saying, "My little daughter is at the point of death. Come and lay your hands on her, so that she may be made well, and live." And he went with him. And a great crowd followed him and thronged about him.
>
> While he was still speaking, there came from the ruler's house some who said, "Your daughter is

> dead. Why trouble the Teacher any further?" But ignoring what they said, Jesus said to the ruler of the synagogue, "Do not fear, only believe." And he allowed no one to follow him except Peter and James and John the brother of James. When they came to the house of the ruler of the synagogue, he saw a tumult, and people weeping and wailing loudly. And when he had entered, he said to them, "Why do you make a tumult and weep? The child is not dead but sleeping." And they laughed at him. But he put them all outside, and took the child's father and mother and those who were with him, and went in where the child was. Taking her by the hand he said to her, "Talitha cumi"; which means, "Little girl, I say to you, arise." And immediately the girl got up and walked; for she was twelve years old. And immediately they were overcome with amazement. And he strictly charged them that no one should know this, and told them to give her something to eat. (Mark 5:21-24,35-43)

God's timing rarely matches ours, and with good reason.

When Jairus falls at the feet of Jesus, he is looking for a miracle. Rather than heading to the synagogue (he knew well) to ask the God he thought he knew, he headed to the carpenter he knew not at all. Jairus asks the Divine Physician to make a house call; earth cried out to heaven, and heaven responded. Note that in the story, however, while Christ heard the request and immediately took route to the home, an unexpected turn of events delayed Christ's response. We would be wise to realize — especially when asking for healing from God — that the timetable is His, not ours. God healed on His timetable, not Jairus's. The famous healing of the woman with a hemorrhage (not included in the passage above) interrupts this story, sidetracking Jesus's direct path to the house of Jairus. Imagine how Jairus must have felt in that moment. Time was of the essence. Jairus had one plan; God had another. God's timing rarely matches ours, and with good reason. God is timeless, and we are not. Jairus wanted God to act immediately; God acted eventually.

Think about that fact for a moment. Did God respond? Yes. Was it the way Jairus would have liked? No. But, was God still faithful? Absolutely.

Let's break down this passage into slightly "smaller" pieces, though, so as not to miss any details the Holy Spirit is offering us. Journey the extra mile, too, after each Gospel line, and contemplate this rich scene in light of your own faith walk.

> *Then came one of the rulers of the synagogue, Jairus by name; and seeing him, he fell at his feet … (v. 22)*

- Do you believe that God knows your name? That God calls you by name and even has your name carved in His hand, promising He will never forget you (see Is 49:15-16)?
- When you look upon the Lord in the Eucharist, do you fall to your knees in worship? Does your genuflection reflect a repetitious habit or a reverent heart?

> *… and besought him, saying, "My little daughter is at the point of death. Come and lay your hands on her, so that she may be made well, and live." And he went with*

him. And a great crowd followed him and thronged about him. (vv. 23-24)

- To "beseech" is more than to ask; it is to implore with urgency and with fervor. Do *you* beseech God? Do you go to Him with urgency and fervor when you pray for others?
- Do we invite Christ into the situation as a last resort or first response?
- Do we seek the laying on of hands — the physical touch of the sacraments in our own life? Do we see the power of prayer and seek it at every turn?

While he was still speaking, there came from the ruler's house some who said, "Your daughter is dead. Why trouble the Teacher any further?" (v. 35)

- Do we trust in the Lord's timing? Do we trust in His plan more than our own?
- Is God still our God even in times of suffering and death?

But ignoring what they said, Jesus said to the ruler of the synagogue, "Do not fear, only believe." (v. 36)

- Do we attempt to put our own shortsightedness and human limits upon the God of the universe?
- Do you trust Jesus when He tells you not to fear? "Do not fear" happens to be the most oft-spoken command in the Bible. Why do you think that is?

- Did you notice that the Lord posits belief (faith) as the antithesis of and antidote to fear in this scene? Why is that, in your opinion?

And he allowed no one to follow him except Peter and James and John the brother of James. When they came to the house of the ruler of the synagogue, he saw a tumult, and people weeping and wailing loudly. (vv. 37-38)

- Why were only Jesus's closest followers allowed to come with Him? Were they more capable of handling the situation than the others?
- Knowing the reality of life after death as well as His own healing power, what was Christ thinking as He looked upon the wailing crowd?

And when he had entered, he said to them, "Why do you make a tumult and weep? The child is not dead but sleeping." And they laughed at him. But he put them all outside, and took the child's father and mother and those who were with him, and went in where the child was. (vv. 39-40)

- Have you or anyone you known ever mockingly laughed at God? Have you ever given up on a person, a situation, or a problem only to have God reduce your smugness to ashes and crush your pride into dust?
- Why did God invite only the Church (designated apostles representing His Church on earth) and the parents into the room? What does this teach us about how the Church and the family

are supposed to work together to walk young souls to heaven?

Taking her by the hand he said to her, "Talitha cumi"; which means, "Little girl, I say to you, arise." And immediately the girl got up and walked; for she was twelve years old. And immediately they were overcome with amazement. (vv. 41-42)

- Note the physical presence of the Lord in this scene. God draws near, takes her hand, and speaks with intimacy. Where do we see God draw near to us — deadened by sin — to call us to life and physically interact with us as Catholics?

- How long did it take God's grace to animate the girl to new life? Why is the adverb "immediately" (used twice) so vital to the scene?

And he strictly charged them that no one should know this, and told them to give her something to eat. (v. 43)

- Why wouldn't Jesus want Jairus to tell *everyone* about what had happened? Why the order of silence?

- Though the girl's spiritual needs were met and her life renewed, she still had basic human needs, physically. What might the command for food to be given foreshadow in the Catholic life?

The Savior in the suffering

Take a moment now and peer into the eyes of Our Lord, once again. Put yourself in the bedroom in Jairus's house.

Which character are you? Are you the apostles, looking with wonder and disbelief at the Rabbi after what He just did? Are you, possibly, the parents wiping away tears of gratitude as you stare into the eyes of mercy? Or are you the daughter, coming to consciousness as you would from a long and deep sleep, the Lord's face slowly coming into focus as you rise? Whichever vantage point you take, the Lord's gaze is the only constant. He is always looking upon us, watching over us, and inviting us to trust Him more perfectly.

Too often we put the timeless one on our time, don't we? Had Jesus made it to Jairus's home with his daughter ailing but still alive, would the miracle have been as "impressive" to those present, or to us reading it so many centuries later? Would Jairus and his wife have been as grateful or as devoted to the Lord if He had merely healed a fever and not raised their child from the dead? I was assuredly more grateful to the doctors in the neonatal intensive care unit for helping my son during a situation of possible death than I am for the doctor who merely listens to a cough and prescribes some medicine. Sure, both are helping, but the situation affects my level of intensity and gratitude. It's human nature, and it's normal. Do we apply the same ferocity to our prayer lives, though?

Oftentimes we hit our knees in prayer most fervently when we are just out of options. Jesus often becomes our last resort, when everything else we try fails. On more than one occasion I have certainly knelt in a nondenominational hospital chapel begging the God of the universe for a favor, a pardon, more time for a soul I loved. Maybe you have, too. Now, to be clear, God welcomes these prayers as He does all prayers. I think God sometimes allows these moments in our lives to offer us — again — the gift of dependence. He wants to be our first and only option. God wants to be the forethought and the afterthought. Prayer offers us that opportunity. It is when we are suffering the most, when we begin to buckle under the weight of the stress or fear or pain, that we must remember prayer is where the cross changes shoulders.

Does God turn a blind eye or deaf ear to our sufferings? Is He somehow "allowing them" to teach us a lesson, to get us to pray more, or to be more appreciative of life? It's in these moments of fear and stress that we often attempt to apply our finite, imperfect thinking to our infinite, perfect Father, which obviously doesn't work. While God does not will our suffering, He allows it at times. God knows well that when His faithful endure the sufferings and trials of this life, it grows them in virtue and in wonder. Our first pope, St. Peter, reminded us:

> *In your hearts reverence Christ as Lord. Always be prepared to make a defense to any one who calls you to account for the* ***hope*** *that is in you. (1 Peter 3:15, emphasis added)*

This verse presupposes something amazing — that no matter what comes our way, joys or sufferings, trials or temptations, life or death — the true Christian is going to be living in such a way that *others will be drawn to our joy and our hope*. Why else would he warn us to "be prepared"? Why else would we need to have our testimony ready? St. Peter is presupposing that you and I are living such joy-filled and exuberant lives, trusting in the providence and loving care of our Father, that people see something "different" in us. People ought to look at us and think: "What are you on?!? How can you still trust God after all you've been through?"

The Gospels, as we have already seen, are an invaluable gift to our faith journey, as they offer us one of the things most sorely lacking in today's world: perspective.

A matter of life and death

Several years ago, my (then) fiancée and I made our way through the frigid streets of Rome one dark January morning. Hoping to beat the crowds, we desired to have some quiet time to pray together in St. Peter's Basilica the day before our wedding.

Upon entering this glorious sanctuary for the first time, we were immediately rendered speechless by the beauty surrounding us. We weren't even ten feet in the door before seeing one of history's most famous works of art, the *Pietà* by Michelangelo.

The statue had always fascinated me. Beyond the incredible artistry and exquisite detail, for me the *Pietà* was an invitation into the heart and mind of God … and Mary. The faithful yet sorrowful mother holding her heroic yet lifeless Son is something to behold. "What a tragic end to a miraculous life," many thought, no doubt, on that eerie Friday afternoon atop Calvary's hill. Of course, as Christians, we have the advantage of looking at Good Friday in retrospect. Twenty centuries later we know that the miraculous end to Good Friday would be revealed on Easter Sunday morning.

As it is with the Christian life, if we want to see clearly as God sees, we have to look at the "big picture" of salvation. If we want to understand Jesus's death, for instance, we need to begin with His birth, and when we do, we will undoubtedly learn something very interesting: that He was born to die.

If you want to get technical, that "pietà" moment first occurred not on Calvary, but in Bethlehem. The manger's wood was a foreshadowing; it is the "cross" of Christmas. There is far more going on at Jesus's birth than many of us initially realize.

At first glance, the Joyful Mysteries of the Rosary might not appear that joyful. Consider these moments from the Gospel: A teenage virgin is pregnant, but not with her husband's child. The girl then leaves home for months alone to go to the hill country and extended family. Later, Mary travels ninety miles by donkey in her third trimester of pregnancy. She gives birth in a cave surrounded by animals, hears from a prophet that both she and her child will suffer greatly, and then, to top it all off, her preteen son — the son of God — goes missing for three days. Most would not consider these moments very joyful. Upon further reflection on these mysterious events, however, you begin to see that they are actually a cause for intense joy.

God was on a rescue mission to save you, and that mission included some courageous souls fighting through some incredibly challenging and painful situations. Not only do the Joyful Mysteries walk us more deeply into the conception, birth, and childhood years of our Lord Jesus, but they reveal to us a God who is madly in love with us, a God who will stop at nothing to save all of us from death.

Mirror images

There's a famous saying that to be successful one must "begin with the end in mind." If that is the case, there is no better example of success than the Gospels. God, quite obviously, had a detailed plan to save us, as the birth and death of Jesus have striking similarities.

Consider just these few parallels between **Bethlehem** and **Calvary**:

- Angels are present during Jesus's birth, death, and resurrection (see Lk 2:13; Mt 26:53; Jn 20:12).
- Mary our Mother is present in both accounts (Mt 2:11-13; Jn 19:26-27).
- In both scenes, Jesus was draped in swaddling clothes (Lk 2:7; 23:53).
- Each event was accompanied by a celestial act/sign (Mt 2:2; 27:45).
- The wooden manger lies between two animals/thieves (Is 1:3; Luke 2:12; 23:33).
- A righteous man named Joseph was present both times (Lk 2:16; Jn 19:38).
- Jesus was pronounced "King of the Jews" at each (Mt 2:2; Jn 19:19).

Both events took place on a hill, on the outskirts of Jerusalem (Bethlehem and Calvary are both set within many hills). Both Jesus's birth and death/resurrection were foretold in advance (prophecy), both were miraculous, and both involved God "emptying" himself for us. And both, ultimately, led to our salvation.

How divine that the same eyes that welled up with joyful tears one starry night in Bethlehem also shed the broken tears of a widowed mother holding the same blessed Body years later. The only thing separating the Nativity from the Pietà is time and perspective. The wooden manger lay in the shadow of a wooden cross. Joseph held and wiped the blood off his new baby boy that night in Bethlehem, and Joseph of Arimathea would share a similar honor three decades later.

Biblical scholars affirm that it was not a barn but a cave hewn out of rock that served as the first Christmas tabernacle, which is a perfect mirror image to the Easter tabernacle of the rock-hewn tomb. It was out of a cave that the Word became flesh and out of a cave that the Word breathed life once again. Both caves acted as a starting point for heaven, although both were "ending points" in the eyes of earth.[1]

Now, some people like to look upon these consistencies as "proof" that the stories must be false or deemed pure myth. That point of view is painfully shortsighted, however, as it fails to respect not only God's providence, but also the irrefutability of written prophecies penned centuries earlier. No, these similarities were part of God's divinely inspired design, showing us all the inseparability of the two events: Christmas and Easter are like two sides of the same coin.

God is not ironic; He is, however, omnipotent, providential, and sovereign (big ways of saying all knowing, all directing, and all powerful). His plan, from the beginning, was to save us. That is why we say that Jesus "was born to die." When God emptied himself and took flesh (see Phil 2:7-9), He was on a mission. Christ came to do for us what we could not do for ourselves. In both of these events, history and the future were both irreversibly changed forever. How fitting that the two main events in this drama we call life would be linked by the same cast of "characters."

Bethlehem and Calvary are less than seven miles apart geographically; they are even closer in the heart of God. Contemplate these things in your heart as you enter into each Christmas season. In Jesus's birth we celebrate His life, which resulted in His death, which offered us all new life … in Him.

So, it seems, that love and suffering are inexorably linked. They certainly were for my wife and me in that hos-

1 *Blessed Are the Bored in Spirit,* Mark Hart (Servant Books).

pital exam room. Perhaps that's why God created us the way He did, so that extreme joy and extreme anguish produce the same physical effect: tears. Maybe it's the Divine Physician's way of offering a higher perspective, demonstrating the inseparable connection between love and suffering.

A Step Beyond

It's easy to allow our prayer to become all about us, but, in doing so, we miss out on an amazing opportunity to draw closer to the mystical body of Christ — in those souls around us and those who have gone before us.

Open to a clean sheet of paper in a journal or open a new document on your computer or tablet. Begin a list of everyone in your life who needs prayers. Begin with those closest to you but extend as far out as you can. Include the souls you've encountered whom you hardly know but who, for whatever reason, the Spirit tapped you on the shoulder about when you interacted with them. It could be the grumpy teller at the bank, the stressed-out barista at the coffee shop, or the clerk who checked you out and simultaneously shared his life story with you because you would listen.

Tonight, rather than petitioning your own prayer intentions, take that list and all of those souls to prayer, asking God to bless them and their intentions. Look to God with an expectant heart and wonder as His closest three apostles did. Look to Christ with hope and gratitude as Jairus and his wife did. And allow the Spirit to open your eyes to the power of Jesus in a new way, as He did to that risen child so many centuries ago.

Chapter 9

Encountering Jesus Unlocks Eternal Life

Christ and Dismas

One evening, while the local news was on the television, the weather report came on. For someone living in Arizona, meteorology is not an exact "science," nor is it exactly fortune-telling. There are only so many ways to say, "It's going to be hotter than Gehenna." This particular night the broadcast got our attention because the forecast called for a chance of rain. During the report, the "meteorologist" (yes, I put that in quotes) said the following day would be "party cloudy," but the weekend would be "mostly sunny." The distinction catalyzed an interesting question from my then seven-year-old: "Daddy, what's the difference between partly cloudy and mostly sunny?"

Not wanting to get into an ill-educated dialogue in which I revealed my true ignorance while bellowing on about cloud density and barometric pressure, I opted for a simpler response: "Well, sweetie, I guess it depends on whether the weatherman is an optimist or a pessimist."

I go back to that moment every time I hear one or the other used in a weather report. We're reminded in Scripture that rain falls "on the just and on the unjust" (Mt 5:45), after all. We will all have good days and bad days: "sunny days" and days filled with life's storms. You can always tell by the look on someone's face if they woke up counting their problems or their blessings. As Archbishop Fulton Sheen said, "The major difference in human beings is not in what happens to them, but in how they react to what happens."

Consider this story of two stonemasons:

> You walk up to the first stonemason and ask, "Do you like your job?" He looks up at you and replies, "I've been building this wall for as long as I can remember. The work is monotonous. I work in the scorching hot sun all day. The stones are heavy and lifting them day after day can be backbreaking. I'm not even sure if this project will be completed in my lifetime. But it's a job. It pays the bills." You thank him for his time and walk on.
>
> About thirty feet away you walk up to a second stonemason. You ask him the same question, "Do you like your job?" He looks up and replies, "I love my job. I'm building a cathedral. Sure, I've been working on this wall for as long as I can remember and yes, the work is sometimes monotonous. I work in the scorching hot sun all day. The stones are heavy and lifting them day after day can be backbreaking. I'm not even sure if this project will be completed in my lifetime. But I'm building a cathedral."[1]

---

1 *Start with Why,* Simon Sinek (Portfolio/Penguin).

It's amazing how perspective changes the more humble we are. Next to forgiveness, ***perspective*** is probably the gift most freely offered by God yet seldom requested. Perspective transforms sadness into joy and calls sinners to sainthood. Perspective shatters despair and replaces it with hope. Perspective is what keeps the modern Christian going while others shake their heads in hopeless disbelief. When it comes to Jesus Christ, perspective offers timely insight into timeless truths.

God was dying not because He lacked an answer to sin, but because we did.

In the previous chapter, we viewed the Crucifixion through the lens of the Nativity. What a difference three decades made. Mary stared into the same face, the same eyes on Calvary's mount as she did on Bethlehem's hills, but the swaddling clothes had been replaced by a loincloth and burial linens. The One who was prefigured in the Old Testament and transfigured atop Mount Tabor was now disfigured and lifeless in her immaculate arms.

Picture God's face bloodied and brutalized. His eyes swelling shut. His speech labored. His scalp protruding sacred blood from the earthly crown emblazoned upon His regal head ... the very same head that Mary and Joseph kissed long ago beneath the same southern Israel sky.

Peer into the tortured eyes looking with forgiveness upon His torturers. Hear the voice of the One who once healed with spit but has now been spat upon. Ponder the sinful irony that the carpenter who used wood to build was now being destroyed by tools — wood, nails, and hammer — that He wielded, daily, in peace. The woodworker was now upon the wood. The Living Water was, again, thirsty. The Good Shepherd had become the Lamb.

God was dying not because He lacked an answer to sin, but because we did.

A tale of two thieves

We hear often about "the good thief" that Tradition names "Dismas," the one who beseeches mercy from Mercy in the waning hours of Good Friday. We know the episode well: one thief, bad, the other, good. This beautiful episode appears only in St. Luke's Gospel yet gives us invaluable insight into both God and Good Friday. St. Luke's insight is only clear, however, when we begin with St. Matthew's Gospel account of the Crucifixion. Listen to what the Spirit breathes to us through the pen of St. Matthew:

> Then two robbers were crucified with him, one on the right and one on the left. And those who passed by derided him, wagging their heads and saying, "You who would destroy the temple and build it in three days, save yourself! If you are the Son of God, come down from the cross." So also the chief priests, with the scribes and elders, mocked him … and **the robbers who were crucified with him also reviled him in the same way**. (27:38-44, emphasis added)

Note that when the crucifixions began, **both** the criminals crucified with him joined in the mockery. There was no "good thief" when the day began, at least not that we saw. The souls on the right and left of the cross saw only condemnation hanging between them. Jesus was obviously no one special, for no true god would allow himself to be butchered and destroyed as this rabbi had been. No one capable of stopping this level of brutality and abuse would endure such pain.

So what changed in the heart of Dismas that afternoon? What happened during those three hours? What did he witness from the one hailed and titled "King of the Jews" as he suffered beside Him? What inspired this bad thief to turn "good" on this Good Friday?

> One of the criminals who were hanged railed at him, saying, "Are you not the Christ? Save yourself and us!" But the other rebuked him, saying, "Do you not fear God, since you are under the same sentence of condemnation? And we indeed justly; for we are receiving the due reward of our deeds; but this man has done nothing wrong." And he said, "Jesus, remember me when you come in your kingly power." And he said to him, "Truly, I say to you, today you will be with me in Paradise." (Luke 23:39-43)

Perhaps it was the gentleness in Jesus's tortured spirit. It may have been the charity in his labored words between gasping breaths. Maybe it was compassion in the sideward glance through bruised, barely open eyes. Whatever it was, it made an impact on Dismas. Hanging in the presence of innocence, his own guilt became all the more clear. As the sky grew dark, the Light shone more brightly. The convict was now convicted that the man in the middle had indeed done nothing wrong.

The revelation is even more illuminating in the dichotomy of dialogue offered between the left and the right. The criminal on the left begins calling Christ out, almost demanding Him to act. His cries are out of self-interest, though, not out of self-condemnation or adoration. "Save yourself, and us!" is the cry of a soul who wants the pain to stop and the sentence reversed. "We are receiving the due reward of our deeds," however, is the cry of a penitent soul, who accepts the pain. "Remember me" is a soul begging to have the sentence not reversed but redeemed. As Archbishop Fulton Sheen so eloquently put it, "The thief on the left wanted to be 'taken down' but the thief on the right wanted to be 'taken *up*.'"

Making sense out of suffering

So, why is suffering and, by extension, Jesus, so "irreconcilable" in this modern culture? Put simply, the modern world cannot stand what it cannot explain or control. Modern culture cannot fathom how it can put a probe on Mars, clone animals in labs, and cure the intimacy problems of eighty-year-olds, but not "solve" the problem of suffering. Sure, we can counsel it, medicate it, run from it, or try to ignore it, but in the end none of those remedies or distractions act as solutions to the purpose of suffering. Suffering makes sense only in Christ. Divorced from Jesus, suffering lacks any purpose.

As Scripture notes and Tradition affirms, when Christ finally died, His holy side was pierced and a stream of blood and water flowed from His side. This holy river signaled the conception of His Church with the blood and waters of God's divine mercy flowing straight out of the altar of the Son's sacred heart. Just as in His carpentry shop, Jesus's blood, sweat, and tears *created* works of beauty, now, they would birth something lasting and eternal, something the netherworld could never topple: one, holy, catholic (universal), and apostolic Church.

In the midst of the blood and water, though, we see where the thief on the left went wrong and where Dismas got it right.

The bad thief wanted the suffering to end but showed neither penitence nor desire to change. "Get me out of this!"

was a plea for the blood of Jesus to heal him, but not for the water of Jesus that would call him to change. Many of us go to God in moments of desperation, looking for healing, but once the suffering is over go back to our own devices. It's as if we are saying: "I want the healing but not the accountability. I'll take your blood if it will make my bleeding stop, but you can keep the water of baptism that would call me out of my own selfish way of life." We want the ER doctor to restart our sin-clogged heart, but not the ongoing prescription for a healthy diet on the Bread of Life.

Others in life prefer the water but not the blood. They want to be part of the Jesus club, to be included as His children and have assurance of salvation. They want the glory of heaven on an earthy throne. We see a glimpse of this when James and John Zebedee approach the Lord, asking a special favor:

> James and John, the sons of Zebedee, came forward to him, and said to him, "Teacher, we want you to do for us whatever we ask of you." And he said to them, "What do you want me to do for you?" And they said to him, "Grant us to sit, one at your right hand and one at your left, in your glory." But Jesus said to them, "You do not know what you are asking. Are you able to drink the cup that I drink, or to be baptized with the baptism with which I am baptized?
>
> "For the Son of man also came not to be served but to serve, and to give his life as a ransom for many." (Mark 10:35-38,45)

It wasn't good enough for James and John to be counted among the Twelve. They wanted even more preferential treatment — they wanted to be No. 1 and No. 1A on the

VIP list. At the time, they still misunderstood the purpose of Christ's mission, which kingdom they were seeking, and the path it took to get there. It's actually quite telling in the Gospel of St. Mark, almost divinely inspired wordplay when the brothers ask to sit "one at your right hand and one at your left, in your glory" as the very next time we hear right and left from St. Mark, it reads:

> And with him they crucified two robbers, one on his **right** and one on his **left**. (Mark 15:27, emphasis added)

The glory of heaven doesn't come without tasting death on earth: death to sin, death to pride, death to self, etc. This is why baptism is so vital, so primary, and so life altering. We are baptized not only into Jesus's life, but also into the Lord's death. Baptism is precisely that — a *death* to this world with the promise of the next. Those who opt for the water but not the blood, though, want the *benefits* of baptism without the risks that comes with it. The problem is that life doesn't work that way. We cannot expect the crown without the thorns, nor the reward without the risk. The streets of heaven may be paved with gold, but the path to heaven is assuredly not (see Rv 21:21; Mt 7:14).

When we, like James and John, fail to understand the point or even the purpose of suffering, when we turn inward on ourselves and not outward toward our neighbor, it's time to repent.

A confession to make

I have a confession to make: most of the time I'm the thief on the left. I'm almost tempting Jesus. I'm yelling at Him. I'm talking to Him as if He's my equal. I come to Him with expectations not that He'll solve my problem, but that He'll solve it my way and on my timetable. It's as if I'm saying, "Hey, if you're really God, do this!" Or, "Hey, Jesus, if you really love me, get me out of [insert impossible situation here]! And if you do, I'll [insert impossible promise here that I'll break in a week]!"

The glory of heaven doesn't come without tasting death on earth.

Yes, I am the thief on the left. Do you know what I want? I don't want His salvation, because that means I'm going to have to change. What I want is His healing. I want Him to make my life right. I want Him to take away the bad things that are happening. I want Him to take away my pain, take away my bitterness, take away my anger, my temptations, fears, and loneliness, and all those other frustrations. "Take them away, God. You can heal me, but you cannot save me," I would say in prayer if I had the courage to actually profess it out loud. We have a lot of patients in our world, in our homes, in our schools, and in our churches — people who go to Christ as healer but fear going to Him as Savior. As soon as we profess we are penitent the game changes, for now our lives will carry with them an expectation to act and live differently. Speaking from experience, if you're going to be a patient, you'd better be a penitent who wants salvation, because Christ won't stop pursuing until you stop running.

It is only when we embrace the water *and* the blood, the joys *and* the sufferings that grace can take effect and do what it is designed to do: bring life. The sacraments are our physical, tangible pathway from death to life. It is in the sacraments that heaven kisses earth with the tender lips of mercy. Properly understood, each of the seven sacraments is an invitation to die to ourselves, our sin, and our selfishness, so that we might live no longer for ourselves, but for Christ (see Gal 2:20; 2 Cor 5:15).

In fact, the final exchange between Dismas and Jesus is, in essence, a foreshadowing of what happens with us in the Sacrament of Reconciliation. A broken soul looks into the eyes of God in the person of Christ, sin laid bare, admits guilt and shame with a penitent heart, begs God for mercy, and receives not only forgiveness but absolution and the promise of eternal life. How different our collective experience would be if we thought of that kneeler in the confessional as the crossbeam, where God transformed sin into grace.

Never, ever forget

The plea of Dismas leads us not only to the Sacrament of Reconciliation but also back to the Eucharistic table the night prior. Consider the two passages from St. Luke's Gospel separated by less than twenty-four hours:

> And he [Dismas] said, "Jesus, **remember** me when you come in your kingly power." And he said to him, "Truly, I say to you, today you will be with me in Paradise." (Luke 23:42-43, emphasis added)
>
> And he [Jesus] took bread, and when he had given thanks he broke it and gave it to them, saying, "This is my body which is given for you. Do this in **remembrance** of me." (Luke 22:19, emphasis added)

It's a fascinating word: remember. In our Western culture, we use it quite figuratively, as in, "to recall with fondness" on an anniversary, or to "call upon data" when heading to the store without a grocery list. For our Hebrew brethren, however, to *remember* meant something far greater.

Properly understood, when the Jewish people said, "remember," it meant to be rejoined to, almost to "become one (member) with again." Far more than a pithy concept or a fond recollection, the Jewish people would view it in a less temporal and more spiritual place, in which time almost stood still. It's for this reason, in part, that God was repeatedly telling the Jews of the Old Testament to "remember" His works and the Jewish writers were constantly begging God to "remember" them! God's children were to "remember" the revelation given them atop Mount Sinai when moving forward in faith or walking in circles in the wilderness.

The miracle of Good Friday is that God didn't call on a miracle.

God knows we will forget all He has done for us. God understands how fickle we can be. This is, I think, one of the reasons for His constant admonition to remember. He wants us not only to recall, but to prayerfully reengage, reencounter, and re-immerse ourselves in the moments when He has revealed His love and faithfulness to us. This is the purpose not only of signs such as wedding rings and sacramentals (such as holy water) but of the sacraments themselves. This is why Jesus bid us to "do this in remembrance" and commanded us to do it, at the least, every week. God *knew* what we needed before we even asked for it. We need to be in His divine presence during the joys and the struggles of life, to offer thanks or seek healing, but always for His glory, just as Dismas rightly did.

The miracle of Good Friday is that God didn't call on a miracle. He mounted that cross and took our place. We sinned, and He was punished; we ran up the bill, yet

He arrived and paid the debt we couldn't pay. We cannot and must not ever forget Who saved whom and Who invites whom to abide in Him. For a grape to offer its blood to make wine, it must first stay connected to the water of the vine. Likewise, for us to bear fruit throughout the season of life — even the droughts — we must be near enough to the Lord to peer into His eyes, to hear His voice, and to "remember" His promise. It was as true for Dismas on the wooden altar of sacrifice as it is for each of us as we advance toward the altar of sacrifice in our local parish sanctuaries.

A Step Beyond

Everyone has a cross to bear. Oftentimes, though, we are so overwhelmed by the weight of our own that we fail to notice the crosses born on the shoulders of those around us, whether beloved friends or annoying "foes." Allow eye contact and intentional presence to be your form of prayer today or for the next few days. Make it a point to turn off your phone and surrounding screens. Make eye contact with everyone with whom you speak. Acknowledge the Spirit of Christ within them. Ask them questions. Validate their feelings. Offer hope for their situations. Affirm their goodness and beauty. See Christ, as Dismas did, in a way others fail(ed) to do.

By your entering into others' sufferings, your own sufferings will find purpose; in humbling yourself, you will be exalted.

Chapter 10

Encountering Jesus Illuminates Your Mind

Christ and Cleopas

I once heard a story about an old farmer who was cleaning out his attic. As he sorted through all the family heirlooms and antiques, the farmer decided to take the dust-covered junk in his attic to sell or discard. He filled his pickup truck and drove to town in hopes of having its value assessed and, possibly, making a few dollars. The boxes were gone through and little was offered. Finally, the surveyor noticed an irregularity on one of the paintings. The corner of the canvas had been scratched, and it revealed not a hole but another canvas beneath. Imagine everyone's surprise when a simple, dusty painting of a bowl of fruit was peeled back to reveal a stunning and priceless work of art from a famous Renaissance artist. The farmer, in shock, screamed with joy and headed back to his farm a very wealthy man. One man's junk is another man's treasure, as they say.

Not everyone you know believes that the Eucharist is truly Jesus's body and blood, soul and divinity. According to statistics, even many Catholics who go to Mass on Sunday don't necessarily believe it, or "aren't sure." But, how about *you*? Gaze into the Lord's eyes now. Picture Jesus offering the blessing and breaking the bread as He did in that Upper Room two millennia ago. Hear Him utter the words of consecration.

What do *you* say that the Eucharist is or, more to the point, *WHO* do you say that it is?

Consider the Eucharist you see and receive at Mass. It doesn't look like bread (at least not any bread you buy at the store). It doesn't really even taste like bread. If you put it under a microscope or examined it in a lab, however, you would find that it is absolutely bread, under a slightly different form.

After the consecration, though, what might look and taste like bread on the surface is far more. Jesus's presence is veiled; Christ's glorified body is there beneath the surface, hidden from our earthly eyes. The bread wafer, once the Holy Spirit descends at the prayer of Christ's priest, now conceals history's greatest and most perfect masterpiece, the Bread of Life, the Son of God. History gives way to mystery, making what was past ever present in the re-presentation, the "re-membering" upon the altar.

Look again, now. Take a closer look beyond the bread and wine to see and behold the Body and Blood. For if the people of Nazareth taught us anything, it's that God could be in your midst, right in front of your face, and you might not recognize Him.

Out of sight, out of mind

The following Resurrection account comes to us from St. Luke's Gospel. Though you've no doubt heard it before, I invite you to read it with fresh eyes, now, asking the Holy Spirit to illuminate your mind and help you to "see" details that perhaps you never have before. Ask yourself the question, "Who or what is being consumed in this story?"

> That very day two of them were going to a village named Emmaus, about seven miles from Jerusalem, and talking with each other about all these things that had happened. While they were talking and discussing together, Jesus himself drew near and went with them. But their eyes were kept from recognizing him. And he said to them, "What is this conversation which you are holding with each other as you walk?" And they stood still, looking sad. Then one of them, named Cleopas, answered him, "Are you the only visitor to Jerusalem who does not know the things that have happened there in these days?" And he said to them, "What things?" And they said to him, "Concerning Jesus of Nazareth, who was a prophet mighty in deed and word before God and all the people, and how our chief priests and rulers delivered him up to be condemned to death, and crucified him. But we had hoped that he was the one to redeem Israel. Yes, and besides all this, it is now the third day since this happened. Moreover, some women of our company amazed us. They were at the tomb early in the morning and did not find his body; and they came back saying that they had even seen a vision of angels, who said that he was alive. Some of those who were with us went to the tomb, and found it just as the women had said; but him they did not see." And he said to them, "O foolish

If the people of Nazareth taught us anything, it's that God could be in your midst, right in front of your face, and you might not recognize Him.

> men, and slow of heart to believe all that the prophets have spoken! Was it not necessary that the Christ should suffer these things and enter into his glory?" And beginning with Moses and all the prophets, he interpreted to them in all the scriptures the things concerning himself.
>
> So they drew near to the village to which they were going. He appeared to be going further, but they constrained him, saying, "Stay with us, for it is toward evening and the day is now far spent." So he went in to stay with them. When he was at table with them, he took the bread and blessed, and broke it, and gave it to them. And their eyes were opened and they recognized him; and he vanished out of their sight. They said to each other, "Did not our hearts burn within us while he talked to us on the road, while he opened to us the scriptures?" And they rose that same hour and returned to Jerusalem; and they found the eleven gathered together and those who were with them, who said, "The Lord has risen indeed, and has appeared to Simon!" Then they told what had happened on the road, and how he was known to them in the breaking of the bread. (Luke 24:13-35)

What did the room look like where they gathered to eat? Imagine night falling over Emmaus that Sunday evening. Picture the torrent of emotion in Cleopas and his companion after the three days they'd just experienced. To have their Lord handed over by their own countrymen, brutally murdered by the Romans, and placed in a borrowed grave under military watch. Consider the hope they felt with the testimony of the women and apostles who ventured to the tomb and the confusion they must have felt as they departed the dangerous city for Emmaus. How puzzled they must have been by the inquisitive stranger who drew near, how shocked at his ignorance of the current events, and, then, how breathless and awe-struck by His command of the Scriptures of old and their context in their own lives.

Their heads must have been spinning while their hearts were burning. It was at this very moment — with *this backdrop* — that the Lord led their hearts, open and unencumbered, to the table. It was only after the soil of their hearts had been tilled that Jesus felt they were disposed to receive the seed of the Word as revealed in God's Eucharist. It was only in the Eucharist that His disciples could truly see, and only empowered by the Eucharist that they could courageously return to the dangers of Jerusalem.

Many questions, one God

This passage is so rich that an entire book could be written on just it alone. There are so many questions that the inquiring mind and humble heart could ask. In fact, during your next Scripture study or journaling time, I'd encourage you to prayerfully consider a few:

- "*That very day*" they fled Jerusalem for Emmaus. Was it out of fear of the Romans? Dejection over losing Jesus? Were they just trying to get away from their problems? Were they looking for a distraction?

- Have you ever felt as if you were "without God"? Have you ever had your hopes and dreams smashed, leaving you depressed? How did you respond?

- Have you ever felt "*God draw near*" to you? Perhaps you realized it only in retrospect, like these two travelers. Has God ever sent someone into your life to meet you in a dark and down place and journey beside you?

- Have you ever had someone share with you his or her experience of God only to have you doubt its reality? Have you ever felt as if others were "closer" to God than you could ever be? Do you feel as if God has to "do more" for you to really believe?

- "He interpreted to them in all the scriptures" (Lk 24:27). Has God sent people into your life to lead you back to Him? Pastors, teachers, grandparents, godparents, catechists, core members who were bold and joyful emissaries of God's truth and His love?

- Does Jesus force himself on those disciples for dinner, or did He need to be invited to stay? Perfect love never forces its way in; it must be invited.

- Do you recognize the fourfold structure — taken, blessed, broken, shared? Where else do we see that in the Scriptures? And within the Holy Mass?

- Have you ever looked upon the Eucharist and "seen" God with the eyes of faith? Why did God wait to reveal His true presence until that moment? What is God trying to reveal to Cleopas and his companion, and, by extension, to us?

- What caused their spiritual "heartburn"? Have the Scriptures ever been opened up for you in a way that turned and "melted" your heart?

- Did you notice the order Jesus followed? First the Scriptures were opened to them, and then they went to the altar table and consumed the bread. Sound familiar?

- "That same hour" they returned to Jerusalem. Why the rush? Why a seven-mile jog immediately after eating? Why the precarious and quite dangerous "run" in the dark? Why couldn't it wait until morning?
- Have you ever had an experience of God *so real* that you just had to share it immediately? Have you ever become jealous or even annoyed at someone else for sharing their testimony of God in their life?

Of all the Gospel stories St. John Paul II used and quoted during his teachings and exhortations, this story was one of his favorites, particularly as it pertained to his vision for youth ministry and young people in the Church. He would encourage all of us — parents and catechists — to draw near to young people, to journey beside them, and to *first ask questions* before offering wisdom. How often and how easily we forget (in our meek and modern efforts at evangelization) to draw near to other souls, ask questions, and really *listen* … not just talk and attempt to indoctrinate.

God constantly meets us where we are and walks us where He desires us to be.

How vital it is that we are constantly seeking the divine perspective on things! We must cry out to God to rescue and save us from our own small-mindedness and reactionary blindness to the ups and downs of life. How essential it is for us to have wise and humble guides to help us along the journey, and how deadly it becomes when we proudly refuse to listen to them. God sends prophets because we need them. He gives messengers to us to communicate His truth in timely ways we can understand. God gives signs and miracles, big and small, for our benefit. God revealed truth in Scripture and instituted His Church on earth because He is more interested in our salvation than even we are!

Put simply, God does the work. God constantly meets us where we are and walks us where He desires us to be. He will travel to the ends of the earth and send angels, prophets, messengers, and servants in His holy name, charged with bringing the faith to the faithless and hope to the hopeless whenever and wherever they need it. God is constantly reaching out to us; we just have the eyes of faith to see it.

Another dark night (of the soul)

The date was April 14, 1912, when, just before midnight, the RMS *Titanic* collided with an iceberg during her maiden voyage from Southampton, United Kingdom, to New York City. As the 53-ton vessel slowly sank into the icy Atlantic Ocean waters, just over 700 souls were able to make their way to lifeboats and eventually survive. For more than 1,500 souls, however, the Atlantic floor would be their final resting place. Many stories, documentaries, and an Oscar-winning motion picture have told the tales, both historic and Hollywoodesque, that are said to have occurred aboard the ship in her final hours.

One story that has been shared by multiple souls who survived that fateful April night centered on a meek, little British priest named Father Thomas Byles who, though given two separate opportunities to board a lifeboat, forwent both in order to hear confessions and pray with passengers sinking to their doom. Eyewitness accounts from the lifeboats spoke of Father Byles's heroism as he gathered passengers of all faiths together on deck for prayer, consolation, and spontaneous baptism. While the *Titanic* sank and the lifeboats dropped, Father Byles stood near hearing confessions, absolving sins, and fulfilling his office and identity not only as a priest of God but as a true father. A father — a good father — does not know how to stop loving. A father does not seek himself. A true father, in the image of God, seeks to love and save his children. In the darkest of hours, in the coldest of places, God's fatherhood was on display — it was being glorified — it was living and active and working for salvation.

True love works for others' salvation.

The perishing souls need not perish. The bodies may have been sinking, but their souls were offered the chance to soar by God's grace and through His Church. Interestingly, in 1912, Easter Sunday fell on April 7. Though the Titanic didn't hit the ocean floor until Monday, April 15, the night it struck the iceberg was Sunday, April 14, the Second Sunday of Easter, known today as Divine Mercy Sunday. While, in time, Divine Mercy Sunday was not yet "initiated," I like to think that in God's timelessness this was far from a coincidence. As Mary reminds us in Luke 1:50:

> "And his mercy is on those who fear him / from generation to generation."

Under the veil of darkness, amidst the shrieks of terror and impending death, God drew near in mercy and compassion. There, in the midst of absolute tragedy, was a priest of God, sent to His children in the hours they needed him most to bring hope and offer God's mercy. The Father sent a son who was a priestly father to His children, to bring the children back home to the Father. When God draws near, as He did on the road to Emmaus, on the deck of the *Titanic*, or in countless confessionals and on altars around the globe each day, His mercy is freely given to those who seek it.

God sends people into our lives all the time. He draws near to us, though we do not always recognize Him. His voice echoes through those who speak hard truth to us, including family, close friends, and Mother Church. The question isn't whether or not God will send you a mentor or guide when you need it. God sends people to us to speak His truth, offer His mercy, and call us out of our sin. He has for centuries, and He won't stop now.

God still sends people, holy people, to lead us. The question is: Will you follow? Will you keep walking with the Lord even when you are downtrodden? Will you continue to move forward — trusting Him and those He sends in His name — even when you do not know the final destination? Will you continue to go to the Eucharistic table and seek His face, peering behind what looks like bread to see the priceless masterpiece of love that breathes underneath?

When it feels as if all is lost, as if your world is slipping away and you're slowly sinking, look for Christ's priest … seek God's grace. Continue to feed your faith and, in time, your doubts will starve to death.

A Step Beyond

If you want something you've never had, you must be willing to do something you have never done. This week, make it a point to have a Eucharistic "encounter" with the Lord outside of Sunday Mass. Rearrange your schedule to catch a weekday Mass one morning or during a lunch hour. Stop by your parish chapel for adoration and just spend some time in the presence of the Lord. Don't feel the pressure to stay an entire hour if you're not accustomed to it. Even fifteen minutes can dramatically change your day and, in time, your very life.

Don't feel the need to talk to the Lord the entire time, either. Be content just to bask in His glory and listen. St. John Vianney — the patron saint of priests — had a particularly strong devotion to the Eucharist and wrote on it profoundly. He was constantly advocating for and encouraging the faithful to spend more time in the presence of Christ in the Eucharist. One famous story he shared was about an elderly man who would regularly come to the saint's parish outside of Mass, sitting in the back of the church, silently staring at the tabernacle for long periods of time. When John Vianney finally asked him what he was doing, the man replied simply, "I look at Him, and He looks at me."

Continue to feed your faith and, in time, your doubts will starve to death.

The Eucharist is deep mystery and high majesty. The Eucharist is also intense simplicity. God comes to us in the simplest of forms (bread), and in the simplest of ways (a family meal, shared among friends). Peer beyond the surface and behold the mystery.

Chapter 11

Encountering Jesus Revealed My True Purpose

Christ and Me

It's odd when the worst day of your life is also the very best day. It seems illogical, really. How can the pit of your sadness and realization of your own depravity and sin coexist simultaneously with the cognition of God's perfect love, divine mercy, and unyielding presence? For anyone who has experienced it, you realize that the two realities are not mutually exclusive. Truthfully, the more keenly aware we become of our own sin, the more glorious the Cross becomes. Christ disfigured is — in truth — far more beautiful than Christ transfigured, for in His brokenness we find worth and value in our own brokenness — and in God's limitless love, for we don't deserve it.

I'll never forget my first conversion experience. I say "first" because I've had countless conversions since. I've grown tired of Hollywoodesque conversion stories, to be honest. The horrible-sinner-to-amazing-saint conversion — with the exception of St. Paul — is just not normal. St. Paul, to be clear, is the exception more than the rule (exemplified by his designation of "saint"). Very few conversions are as larger than life or as outwardly stark. But, the enemy has led many of us to believe that these types of conversions are the litmus test, the pole-vault bar we must clear if our own personal conversion story or testimony is to measure up. At the risk of mixing metaphors (which I have happily done chapter after chapter), the Way of the Cross does not call us to pole-vault over others' bars but, rather, to become so small — to decrease, as St. John the Baptist would put it (see Jn 3:30) — that we might limbo underneath, instead.

Very few, if any, conversion stories span the moral or spiritual pendulum as St. Paul's did. Most of us are far too oblivious, far too stubborn, far too easily distracted and self-involved to fully "convert" after just one run-in with God's grace. No, in the Nativity set of life, I'm more the ox than the angel, more the ass than a wise man. I would expect for at least some of you reading this, conversion is a multi-step and ongoing process, in which our stubbornness forces the Lord not only to repeatedly demonstrate His unconditional love and unyielding patience, but also to get "creative" in how He gets our attention.

I had everything in the world figured out at sixteen. Lucky for me, though, God intervened, and for this smug teenage soul who had everything to lose, socially, and seemingly nothing to gain, thank God He did. For the heart that had told God, "Show me something *big*, if You are real …" the Lord responded by becoming *small*.

Sixteen and stupid

I can still recall every facet of the room in the dimly lit retreat center. My mother had forced me to go on retreat as the final step of my confirmation preparation. I boarded a bus against my adolescent will and was carted hours away to what I considered hell on earth under the guise of a Christian retreat center.

There, nestled tightly between the fir trees, in a lakeside cabin — a setting reminiscent of every clichéd horror film — my worst fears were realized. The smell of burnt grilled cheese from a Knights of Columbus volunteer cook filled the room in which we were. The tongues of fire that descended this fine day were not pentecostal, as our cook crew shrieked in terror at the grease fire that at one point I'd hoped would consume me. Still, the stench of burnt food and Lysol filled the air, and I sat uncomfortably upon my carpet square on a cold cement floor, feigning interest in talk after talk and skit after skit. I found the youth minister dorky, the musician annoyingly exuberant, and my small group uninspiring. If *this* was the best the Church had to offer, Lord, "no wonder so many leave," I thought to myself.

No, in the Nativity set of life, I'm more the ox than the angel, more the ass than a wise man.

Session after session, my disdain grew. I went from not contributing to being negative. Rather than be mute in small-group discussions, my hard heart began to shine forth. I questioned God's existence and challenged my leader to prove me wrong. I openly mocked other teens — far braver than I — who were sharing their own experiences of God's love (which I secretly desired but could never admit). When the group sang songs aloud, I shook my head in self-professed superiority. When they prayed, I yawned. When they opened their hands and hearts, my hands went into my pockets as I used every fiber of my physical being to recoil and, thus, "exert" my physical dominance and independence. And, by the time Sunday morning rolled around, everyone on that retreat was ready to offer me as the closing sacrifice. Luckily for me, God had other sacrificial plans on the (not-so-hidden) agenda.

It was Sunday morning, and the closing Mass began. Our pastor, who had driven up to meet the group, entered the room wearing his typical priestly dress (I had no idea what an alb was or what it signified) and began his normal routine. He kissed the makeshift altar, offered a blessing, and encouraged our hyperactive and hormonal teenage souls to listen to the readings I was sure had nothing to do with my adolescent angst. He offered a homily I don't remember but he certainly seemed to believe in. He spent what seemed like an eternity moving that little ribbon in the big book on the altar, trying to find the appropriate prayer. "Who keeps moving the ribbon on these guys?" I laughed to myself. It was a funny idea … one I wished I'd thought to do. Basically, it was a typical Mass. Readings were read, the homily was dead, and the music left more than a little to be desired. It was proof to me that if Mass were, indeed, God's idea, then His divine "plan" to save us from death was, first, to bore me to it.

Nothing in the universe could have prepared me for what happened next.

The priest took the bread and gave thanks. Father then took the bread and uttered a prayer, the same prayer I'd heard countless times before at Mass. Little did I know the prayer was from sacred Scripture, nor would I have cared at that point. The Holy Spirit — the author of Scripture — picked this day to introduce me to the power of the Living Word of God.

"Take this and eat of it … for ***this is my body***," the priest exclaimed.

It was a prayer I'd heard thousands of times, one that had never really caused me a second thought, but for one split second on this random Sunday morning in a back-woods retreat center, I stopped looking inward and, instead, gazed upward.

In that one second, my soul asked the question that my mind feared to ask: "What *if? What if that is* ***really God?*** *What if that is really what Father says it is? What if that is really* ***Who*** *he says it is?* ***What if?!?***"

That was all it took. That was all the Holy Spirit needed … in one second of openness, one second of profound humility, I opened the door to my heart just a crack, and the Carpenter from Nazareth wedged His sandal in the opening of the door, never to let it shut again.

God drew near.

The sinner who'd longed for and searched for a Savior in all earthly manners and varying intellectual ways had finally come to a crossroads only to find the cross-bearer at its intersection. In that moment, everything else faded. I couldn't hear the music. I couldn't hear the prayers. It was as though I was overwhelmed by the reality of God's existence, His mercy, and His unfathomable love. It was as though Jesus came really close, pulled me really close into Him, looked me deep in the eyes, and said, "*You're mine … and I'm never letting you go.*"

Overcome, I buckled against the back wall of the retreat house. Fighting back tears and gasping for air, I found that my entire world had been upside down; Christ came and razed my temple, leaving all of my false gods scattered in His path and a hope-filled future before me. It *is* truly odd when the "best day" and "worst day" of your spiritual life occur concurrently. It was with this backdrop that the God of the universe wrecked *my life* and left only His grace in its place … and I will thank Him until my dying breath that He did.

No turning back

God has a funny way of showing up when you least expect it but most need it. Just ask Noah, or Abraham, or Isaac, or Rachel, or Joseph, or Moses, or Joshua, or Ruth, or David, or Elijah, or Esther, or Isaiah, or Mary, or Joseph, or Peter, or the woman at the well … you get the idea.

While I can't tell you that everything following the retreat was easy, or that I've never turned away from the Lord, what I can say is that since that day, I've always known (even when I pretended not to) that God was real. This was the first of five hundred or so conversions for me, actually, each one stemming from that first encounter when I opened my heart and God made it personal. Sure, our relationship had begun years earlier when He called me His son, but it was on this morning that the son came seeking the Father, when earth sought heaven and heaven reached down, once again, in the Mass to lift me up and look me in the eyes.

On those days when darkness envelops me or when evil whispers to me, or spiritual attacks surround me, I go back to that moment when I looked into Jesus's eyes … and I **take *a second look***.

I go back to that moment when I was surrounded by wise men (Chapter 1) — those sage guides — but didn't understand why. I recall all the times, actually, that God met me at the well of my shame (Chapter 2) and beside the sea of my frustration (Chapter 3), not merely to fill my hunger but to miraculously exceed my needs (Chapter 4). I think back to those times I sought the loophole over the Lord in my quest for eternal life (Chapter 5), when I was overwhelmed He would choose me (Chapter 6), and how His mercy called me to love and serve Him with everything (Chapter 7). It's when Jesus is my only hope that I pursue Him, again, trusting that He will make sense of my sufferings (Chapter 8).

Yes, it is when I "re-member" the Lord that He remembers me upon His cross (Chapter 9), promising me life eternal. I "re-member" the Mass that Sunday morning and how God was made known *to me* in the breaking of the bread (Chapter 10).

I've needed that memory so many times in the days and years that followed. When I left that retreat it became clear that to foster the change that had taken place within me spiritually, I would need to make some changes around me physically. I had to make some major changes in my life if I really wanted to become who God had designed me to be … so change I did. I broke up with my girlfriend. I quit my raucous party life. I cleaned up my language, began respecting my parents, and, overall, changed my entire attitude.

I shared Christ with my friends — a move that quickly revealed how few friends I really had (see Sir 6:14). I got more involved in my church and changed the music I listened to and the movies I watched.

I learned to pray.

I began going to adoration, bought a Bible, and asked someone far smarter than I to teach me how to read it. I pulled out the rosary I'd been given years earlier at my first Communion and prayerfully rolled those beads until my fingers almost bled. (Someone should have warned me what happens to your heart when you get "Mom" involved, by the way.) The Holy Spirit turned my world upside down, and many of those within it decided they wanted nothing to do with me or my newfound best friend named Jesus.

So, there I was, alone on many weekend nights, trying to be a "good person." No one had told me what would happen if I got serious about following God. No one had told me that there would be really lonely nights sometimes.

No one told me that the devil would come after me harder than ever, trying to distract me from my newfound relationship with Christ (see Rom 7:21).

With true conversion comes freedom but rarely popularity. Here's the part of the story where Hollywood would give us the magical happy ending, right? Where the phone rang and teens from my youth group invited me out, or where my parents came in and we had a great discussion about life and death and God and eternity, right?

Nope. No fairy-tale ending … not for a while. I was lonely, but little did I know God was allowing it for a reason. I needed that time to grow in character and in virtue. He separated me from some bad influences and tempting relationships in order to strengthen me. He had invited me out of the sinful surroundings, sure, but God wanted to transform the desires of my sinful heart.

After a while I developed new friendships — true friendships — the kind that include people who stand with you, walk with you, and challenge you to become a better person. I realized that God hadn't called me to be a "good person" or a "better version of Mark," but a *new* person (see Gal 2:20), one who could fulfill the design He had for me (Eph 2:10).

With true conversion comes freedom but rarely popularity.

In time I realized how important it was for me to feel that loneliness for that season of my life, to learn how to lean on Christ and not just on my friends. I'd been betrayed, gossiped about, mocked, and abandoned, just like Jesus, but not nearly to the same degree. No one in my life, except Christ, could really understand me or the person He was re-creating me to be.

Looking back now, it seems like forever ago that God drew near and "began" walking with me. The truth is that

He was always there; my eyes were just prevented from seeing it. I can honestly say that I can't imagine my life without Jesus Christ — I wouldn't even want to. In Jesus, I've experienced more freedom and joy than I can even begin to express.

If you know it, you know to relish it. If you've had that moment when you've given God that "second look" and realized He has never taken His eyes off you, then you know well what I'm talking about.

If you haven't had that experience, though, or if you're "not sure" you have, I'd like to offer you a moment. The God of the universe has something to say to you and only to you. If you are at a place in your life where you're tired, where you're doubting, where you're straining to trust or afraid to hope, or just exhausted from trying to do it your way ... if you're ready to take "a step beyond" then turn the page.

Chapter 12

Encountering Jesus Calls You to Greatness

Christ and You

Somewhere in your home there are probably baby pictures. They might exist in photo albums or, worse yet, on a shelf, waiting for all to see and good-heartedly mock those in the photos at the next holiday or family gathering. Suddenly, you find yourself wishing you had no childhood, or at least no photographic evidence of one. There you are, diaper-clad, rolls of baby fat, and a future full of hope.

Those pictures tell a story about you, however, and about your earthly beginnings. There might even be ultrasound pictures in an album somewhere lest we forget that your life began nine months before you exited the womb. You had a beginning. God knit you in your mother's womb; we are told that in Scripture (see Ps 139:13-16). He had a design for you and a purpose for you from the beginning (Jer 1:4-8), and that plan is for you to do good works (Eph 2:10).

The point is that God was there from the beginning. You were His creation. He allowed your earthly parents to participate in the very act of creation with Him. Those pictures of you in the hospital celebrate your *natural* birth. You were a creation of God, made in His own image (see Gn 1:26-27). Turn a couple of pages more in that baby album, however, and you'll likely see another "birthday" — the one in which God made you His own child, through the *supernatural birth* at your baptism.

Just like Jesus

The Gospel of Mark doesn't tell us anything about Jesus's childhood or earthly "beginnings." Unlike Matthew or Luke, St. Mark doesn't begin in Bethlehem with the baby in the manger but, rather, with an already adult Jesus heading to the River Jordan.

Jesus wanted to be baptized, though He didn't need it (as He already was the Son of God). He did it to offer us an example, a living witness of what *we needed* to live as a child of God.

What the Holy Spirit describes in just three verses through St. Mark's pen is striking:

> In those days Jesus came from Nazareth of Galilee and was baptized by John in the Jordan. And when he came up out of the water, immediately he saw the heavens opened and the Spirit descending upon him like a dove; and a voice came from heaven, "Thou art my beloved Son; with thee I am well pleased." (Mark 1:9-11)

This scene is the first time we hear God the Father speak in the Gospels, which is noteworthy. What God has to say is important not only for Jesus to know but for us to hear. Jesus is God's Son, which God makes clear here with His own voice. Can you imagine what that sounded like?

God is pleased with Jesus, we learn. Not that it was a news flash. Right now you might be thinking, "Of course, He's proud. How could He not be? Jesus is the perfect kid … literally."

I've found that, in my life, when it's most difficult to pray is when I most need to do so.

Remember, though, that Jesus hadn't "done" anything in public ministry yet. God's love of Jesus was not based on His perfection or His "performance" but on His person. It was the way Jesus loved that caught God's attention. The love the Father had for His Son was not based on His resume; it was rooted in their relationship.

I've witnessed this passage, these three little verses, reduce grown men to sobbing wrecks on a retreat setting or a mission night. It's far easier for us to believe God loves Jesus than it is to believe that God truly, unconditionally, and eternally loves *us.* The key to our relationship with God growing or dying is prayer. Make no mistake, prayer does not merely help our relationship with God; prayer *is our relationship* with God!

I've found that, in my life, when it's most difficult to pray is when I most need to do so. When things haven't panned out the way expected, when sickness sets in, when financial stress becomes overbearing, when marriages end and family members move away (physically or emotionally), that is when we need to position our knees on the floor and refocus our eyes on the Eucharist, again.

I'd like to ask you to pray with me, now.

He's coming for you

Find a quiet space. Create some room for God to breathe and for you to exhale.

Once you do, pray this prayer (slowly):

Come, Holy Spirit.
Come, Holy Spirit.
Come, Holy Spirit.

Holy Spirit, come and fill this place.
Holy Spirit, come and be with me, now.
Holy Spirit, come and dwell within me.

Holy Spirit, I give you permission to work in my life.
Holy Spirit, I give you permission to reveal my shame.
Holy Spirit, I give you permission to love me.

Come, Holy Spirit, dwell within my heart.
Come, Holy Spirit, shake my soul.
Come, Holy Spirit, reveal to me all you wish to show me this day.

Now, picture yourself sitting alone in a chapel. Perhaps it's the chapel at your local parish or a side chapel of the church where you grew up. Place yourself within it. Take a minute to take in the artwork. Note the windows, the icons, the type of floor, the architecture, the colors and shapes that surround you. Feel the seat beneath you. Is it a padded chair or a hard pew? Move your attention before you now and focus in on the tabernacle. Pay attention to its detail, its imagery and design. Note the subtle but consistent flicker of the red candle, the constant yet soft reminder of God's enduring presence among us (see Mt 1:23; 28:20).

Take in the silence in the chapel. If there are exterior noises around you, push them out. Focus on the candle burning beside the tabernacle. Whenever you feel yourself distracted by exterior noises or interior thoughts, just pray, "Come, Holy Spirit" until the distractions dissipate.

Now, a door opens to the chapel and someone enters. Don't turn to look; stay locked on the tabernacle. You hear footsteps moving down the aisle, but you're focused. You hear the steps stop, but you don't look away. Your eyes are fixed on the Lord in His earthly dwelling.

The body who has entered chooses to sit in your row, right beside you. Assuming it must be a family member or close friend, you avert your eyes just for a moment from the Lord and realize *the Lord*. Christ is seated beside you.

Now, I want you to experience the Lord's presence. Sense Him near you.

This is your moment. This is your chance to speak. Trust Him. Pour out your heart. What is it you most desperately want to say or ask or tell the Lord in your life right now?

How would you start?

"Why, Lord, did you ..."

"Why, Jesus, didn't you ..."

"How could you ..."

"Can you still ..."

Whatever is in your heart, whatever you've said a thousand times before, or whatever you've never had the courage to utter aloud, now is your chance. If you want to scream, go ahead ... He can take it. If you need to vent, proceed. If you have questions, ask them. If you are overwhelmed to a point you cannot speak, the Lord is fine with that, too.

If it helps to journal your thoughts, do so. If you need to put down the book and spend time in silence, even better. Allow the Spirit to lead you. Trust in His guidance and in the Lord's mercy.

Once you've had your chance to speak, focus in on Christ once again. Really draw near to Him. Lean into His grace; Jesus has something He wants to say to you. Let Him speak. What would the Lord say to you?

Perhaps it might begin:

"My child, I've never left you …"

"Would I ever abandon you?"

"I died for you …"

"I've forgiven that sin…. I've forgiven you …"

"This is not the life I desire for you …"

"I want to give you more …"

"Will you stop running?"

"Will you let Me love you completely?"

What is the Lord saying to your heart, now?

Is the Lord condemning you or inviting you to something greater, something deeper, something higher?

Sit with Him. Fix your eyes on the Lord. Let Him have the last word.

After a few moments, the Lord rises from the seat beside you. Do you sense that tug in your heart? Do you feel that pull in your chest, hoping He won't leave? Listen to His promise to be with you, always. Now return your focus to the tabernacle. Zoom in on the red sanctuary candle's flicker. Close your eyes and focus on the flicker.

God is now here.

Ever forward

Have you heard God calling you to make some changes across any of these pages? Has the Spirit taken you back to an encounter with God from your past or, possibly, revealed a way God has been trying to get your attention in the present. What now?

Do you remember from the introduction what "every good story has"? Both the greatest stories and the darkest times in history all have one thing in common: they produce the greatest heroes. Christ's story was on display here. Your story is still being written. The world needs the person God created you to be.

Even if everyone else is against you, you still have Christ. He is available to you every second of every day. He is speaking to you in His Word. He is present to you in His Church. He is available to you at every Mass. He promised, "I am with you always, to the close of the age" (Mt 28:20). You are never alone. The good Father could never abandon His children. The Father has never had to give you "a second look," because He has never once taken His eyes off you.

The world needs the person God created you to be.

To the Lord, "even the hairs of your head are all numbered" (Mt 10:30). He has "graven you on the palms of my hands" (Is 49:16). He will "wipe away every tear" (Rv 21:4). He delights in you, He sings over you (see Zep 3:17). He died for you, rose for you, and abides in you (Jn 15:4).

If you believe that the Holy Spirit dwells within you — as Christ promises — then you have no reason to doubt or underestimate your power. It's time to pour out some heroism on a world desperately in need of it. Allow the Holy Spirit to unleash the greatness of your soul.

May your life reflect God's glory, each day, until He calls you home to Him.

Amen.